Balboa Press books may be ordered through booksellers or by contacting:

Balboa Press
A Division of Hay House
1663 Liberty Drive
Bloomington, IN 47403
www.balboapress.com
844-682-1282

ISBN: 979-8-7652-5276-5 (sc)
ISBN: 979-8-7652-5275-8 (e)

Library of Congress Control Number: 2024910933

Print information available on the last page.

Balboa Press rev. date: 08/22/2024

BALBOA.PRESS
A DIVISION OF HAY HOUSE

Happiness

IS AN INSIDE JOB

PLAYBOOK

Reviews and Endorsements

"Ria Flannagan has written and constructed a beautiful book that exudes love and compassion for the reader. It affirms aspects of self while reflecting on the many parts of your life, vulnerabilities, and strengths. As a gifted therapist, Ria's talent shines as she poses beautifully scripted questions and guides the reader through a process of letting go of fears and finding happiness within."
Claudia Black, PhD. Addiction and trauma specialist.
Author of Undaunted Hope and Unspoken Legacy

"I love this book! The daily and weekly exercises meet multiple ways of learning and integrating self-awareness into beautiful direction and transformation!"
Dr. Candace Jordan LAc DACM

"Throughout my nursing background in patient care, ranging from pediatrics to geriatrics within a mental health care setting, I find this workbook to be a valuable resource. The notion of happiness holds significant importance not only for an individual's spiritual and mental welfare but also for their physical well-being. Addressing past trauma is essential for optimal health. This workbook serves as a crucial tool in facilitating wellness and the pursuit of happiness."
Dana Thomas BS, LPN

"Ria Flanagan has woven together a lovely and vibrant workbook designed to open and expand self-knowledge and find true happiness within. The book is laid out with a helpful combination of meaningful psychoeducation and highly impactful exercises so the reader can work on daily bites of significant work and not feel overwhelmed. She caringly explains how and why the exercises are important and has clear direction on where the reader is going next. The material is thoughtful and digestible and is a fantastic way to start a journey of knowing yourself deeper. As a therapist, I would recommend this workbook to my patients as a way to explore who they are, what they want, and work on the obstacles that block them from happiness. The exercises ask effective questions in a relatable manner and the book makes it easy to go at the pace that works best for the reader. The diversity and depth of material is the stuff of change, and the approach is open-minded and fun. This book can change people's lives."
Rebecca Stokes LCPC, CSAT, SEP, EMDRIA Certified Consultant

"Unlock your true potential with Happiness is an Inside Playbook. As a therapist, I've seen firsthand the incredible value of Ria's work with her clients, and this book feels like a heart-to-heart conversation. It helps you ditch limiting beliefs, embrace self-compassion, and tap into your limitless creativity. Through practical advice and inspiring insights, you'll learn to honor your worth, manifest your dreams, and cultivate meaningful connections. Embark on this journey of self-discovery and personal growth, and discover the happiness that comes from within."
Patricia Plum, LCSW

"Ria truly embodies the role of a healer, and this book is evidence of that. From setting intentions to practicing gratitude, Ria understands the keys to inner growth and healing. With over 20 years of experience as a therapist myself, I believe this book will be a valuable resource for my clients for years to come. Thank you, Ria, for creating this exceptional masterpiece of a book!"
Haley Bell MS LISAC, CCTP, CPATP, ACIC, KAP

*Dedicated to my children,
Jaxon and McKayla, my experts in Play
and Happiness.*

Written by
Ria Flanagan

Edited by
Abby Hale and
Devin Flanagan

Design by Ellia
Marcum, Ria
Flanagan

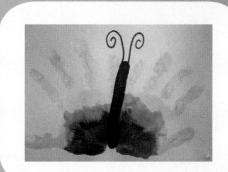

Acknowledgments

I want to thank my husband for editing this workbook with me and my children for inspiring me to dig deeper and heal further, which meant working through more trauma and feeling more uncomfortable feelings to become a better partner, mother, and friend. I want to thank my parents for giving me life, the universe for having my back, and the mentors who taught me and encouraged me. I want to thank Claudia Black and The Meadows for sending me to Onsite in Tennessee for experiential training and to IITAP for CSAT training. I want to thank EMDRIA for EMDR training and Dr. Peter Levine for creating Somatic Experiencing. I want to thank Pia Mellody, who created Post Induction Therapy and wrote about Love Addiction and Codependency. I want to thank the artist PINK for putting on a fantastic concert with her daughter singing on stage next to her, a reminder that there is not only one way to raise children or be a parent, but the common factor is love! We get such a short ride on this planet, and I am so grateful to have shared it with all who have inspired and mentored me. This book is not meant to replace therapy or coaching but as a supplement to invoke mindfulness and connection to self. Happiness in an Inside Job_Playbook is a whimsical, thought-provoking journey to pulling back the layers into the authentic self, moving past conditioning that has numbed out our emotions and stuffed our creativity to unlock the playful spontaneity that is our birthright.

Table of Contents

Table of Contents

Table of Contents

Table of Contents

Note From The Author

I want to thank every single client, reader, friend, teacher, peer, partner, heartbreaker, student, supervisee, supervisor, mentor, therapist, coach, author, director, painter, musician, singer, songwriter, dancer, magician, poet, and my spiritual sandpaper – you have all played a part in who I am today, and for that, I am grateful for you all!

with love, Ria Flanagan

My story is relatable to some and may seem like a terrible adventure to others. In summary, I survived living on my own at 14 years old after a series of traumas had me no longer trusting adults. I was raising myself in dangerous places with other resilient humans, also trying to thrive after many sad stories of not fitting into the "norm." I found a safe place inside of myself that I refer to as intuition to keep me alive. Now, after receiving my Masters in Clinical Psychology emphasis in Marriage and Family Therapy from Pepperdine and currently a doctoral candidate at UAGC paired with the experience of working as a counselor at a psychiatric hospital for trauma and addiction, a clinical director and owner of a private practice I can share with all of you the helpful tools I have gathered through this incredible like journey. I found books and education to be an opportunity to change my circumstances and give back and I truly wish for peace within each one of you with the greater goal of peace on earth! When we change within ourselves the world changes around us. Please join me on a choose your own adventure journey to increase happiness and savor the simple moments that make it all worth it!

Measuring HAPPINESS

Researchers use a combination of different scales to measure happiness levels in people, cultures, and countries. A recent study contributes to our understanding of psychological well-being correlated with having a life purpose (Martela et al., 2024). Another study correlates having and achieving goals is linked to happiness, (Supplemental Material for Happiness—to Enjoy Now or Later? Consequences of Delaying Happiness and Living in the Moment Beliefs," 2021a). What if, for the sake of the time you are reading this playbook, the goal was to increase your baseline level of happiness? By spending time implementing the activities and doing a daily check-in to observe your level of satisfaction, you can track your progress over the next 90 days. People in treatment say it takes at least 90 days to create some new habits or break some old ones, so let's start now. I read my first coaching book by Dan Millman at 16 years old and it expanded my world.
BOOK SUGGESTION: The Life You Were Born to Live -by Dan Millman

HAPPINESS PLAYBOOK
SATISFATION SCALE

0 = not satisfied with
my life today

1 = not really satisfied with
my life today

2= a bit satisfied with
my life today

3= satisfied with
my life today

4= fully satisfied with
my life today

The activities in this playbook were designed to support the reader in an immersive experience of knowing the inner self. With this wisdom, you can create meaningful goals and shift further toward your life purpose. Research correlates having a life purpose with increases in happiness levels. On the road to inner lightness, we may endure some inner darkness, which helps us appreciate the lightness even more.

Setting yourself up to succeed...

Playbook Activity:
Is there a different way you measure happiness or satisfaction in your life that works best for you? If so use that measurement through this process. Write it down for accountability:

Brainstorm ways you measure when things are going well:

What conflict resolution tools do you use to improve circumstances when things need improvement? If you notice you need more tools check out link below and write out a scenario you could use Ed Muzio Perceptual Position:

Tip: check out Ed Muzio concept of Perceptual Position on YouTube:
https://www.youtube.com/watch?v=OCXu1EsS988

Creating INTENTION

There are days when the goal may just be getting through the day, and having a mindset of "I can do this" is enough. Remembering that it is one day at a time, one moment at a time, and using mindfulness to stay in the present moment can support us from future tripping over things we are powerless over.

From the moment we wake up, setting the intention that supports you in having your best day is key. This may change dramatically if a crisis or an illness occurs. Some examples:
- I will accomplish my goals today!
- I will spend some time being creative today.
- I will eat healthily and exercise.
- I can stay in the present moment.

I will remember to say my affirmations during the day (specific to you). These are "I am" statements that combat any negative thoughts or beliefs you may be working through; "I am lovable," "I am worthy," and "I am enough" are very common. Affirmations like "I am safe" can be helpful when feeling anxious (as long as you are, in fact, safe). I will stay grateful for all I have and notice the abundance in my life (food, shelter, family, health) instead of focusing on what I do not have.

I will take the time to let loved ones know how important they are. I will let myself feel my feelings, set healthy boundaries, and use direct communication. I will pay attention to the miracles around me and notice nature's gifts.

If crisis or ill health is an issue, the intention may vary:
Example: "Today, I will take care of everything the best I can and give myself grace."

It can be helpful to permit yourself to ask for help. "I give myself permission to ask for help."

After a crisis or a difficult day, permit yourself to rest. "I give myself permission to rest."

Staying in the present moment can help us avoid the "what if" game since we cannot change the past.

Creating mindful playfulness...

Creating Daily Intentions......

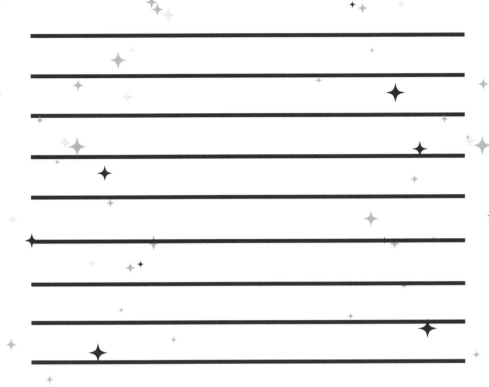

Creating INTENTION

Creating mindful intent in daily living is key to success. Be the creator in your life story!

In the next activity, you will create a safe space to deepen your creativity and intuition. I developed my own when taking a Mindscape workshop from John Veltheim's Bodytalk system.

Using my creation station daily, I was inspired to create something my clients could use for just a few minutes daily. Take a few deep inhales through the nose and out through the mouth to relax before you begin. Provide yourself with a calm, quiet space to prepare. Setting the stage for success with your visualization and have fun with the creative process. If you can commit to daily practice, this can become a powerful space of creation to brainstorm your next life venture.

Building Your Creation Station

1. Close your eyes as you count backward from 8 as you visualize walking toward your workshop/office. Maybe you are walking downstairs or up a mountain path as you count down.

2. Picture this as a top-secret space where no one can get but you. This is a safe space where you are protected, so create any kind of security measures you need.

3. As you walk through the entrance to your workshop, picture a white light washing through you that is healing and restorative, clearing any creative blocks or stressors.

4. Create a space with a computer, TV, or film screen (like a mini theater), where you can spend time brainstorming and projecting images about how you want your future to look. You can also come into this room to ask questions and see what comes on the screen, creating space for creativity and answers to come through to you. This will help strengthen your intuition through creating time and space to practice listening and be open to the messages, images, and symbols, all positive and supportive in nature.

5. You can add a time portal to visit historical places and times, speak to wise masters andguides, and meditate on mountain tops.

Start with going to this space for 5 minutes in the morning and 5 minutes in the evening. In time, you may find yourself spending a few minutes several times a day in your workshop to center, ground, and check in with your intuition. Take a few deep breaths and check in to see what you need in this space today. Have fun building your very own dream workshop! In this sacred space, you will work on practicing intentional gratitude.

**Check out workshops to enhance creativity and intuition: Mindscape
https://www.bodytalksystem.com/**

Brainstorm or draw additional add-ons to your workspace in the circles or use a larger piece of paper and go wild with building your intuitive workspace:

Incorporating Gratitude

Did you know that gratitude is one of the best and most natural ways of increasing your levels of happiness?

Studies show that we all have a baseline level of happiness that we return to after major events. There was a study done on people that won the lottery vs. people that lost the use of their legs (Brickman et al., 1978). As expected, the people that won the lottery were initially happier. The people that lost their legs were initially worse off, but over time, both sets of groups returned to their original baseline of happiness. If we want to move our baseline of happiness, we have to make different choices daily, and gratitude is a game changer to help increase happiness. There is a practice of receiving and holding joy that expands our ability to be with the positive sensations of happiness. When we notice all that we already have and sink into that peaceful place with thoughts of, "I am enough and I have enough" we can slow down and just be for a moment.

As you wake up and enter your workshop, begin by practicing gratitude. List 10 simple things you are grateful for (examples: the air I breathe, a roof over my head, food in my fridge, loved ones, my job, my children...) Practice gratitude as a way of life! Being in gratitude creates a feeling of abundance and can help us be more present in our lives; it is also a way to increase happiness (and who doesn't want more of that!). Try starting the day with a mantra (mind tool) of gratitude. Make a choice to stop being in a "lack mentality" and start noticing all that is going well for you. Start with a simple statement, "I choose to be in gratitude today." Watch as you build and manifest abundance in your life as you change you are empowered to create and choose your thoughts. Play with this thought "I am grateful for this moment of happiness" conjure up a happy moment from the week and now stay with it, breath into it, and notice the sensations. Give yourself permission to feel the sensations of joy, and practice this throughout the day, be playful be gentle to yourself as you try on new routines and practices, it can be like learning to ride a bike. There is humility in the awkwardness of change that is rewarding, it connects us to each other in our vulnerabilities.

Book to help enhance gratitude: The Magic, by Rhonda Byrne

10 Things I am Grateful for Daily

Connection
TO SELF

How do I nurture myself today, in this moment?

Start with a connection to what is happening in your physical and mental being. Checking in with yourself concerning wants, needs, and emotions. Taking care of oneself includes eating healthy, getting adequate sleep, exercising, and feeling the feelings that come up during the day. If emotions are overwhelming to process, or eating and sleeping are an issue, it is vital to seek help from doctors or mental health professionals to get tools to support you in living a healthy lifestyle. You can use the popular recovery acronym H.A.L.T (Hungry, Angry, Lonely, Tired) to check in and connect to the self (body and mind) to assess your wants and needs: Hungry? (If so, make a healthy meal and set reminders on your phone to take breaks to have snacks.) Angry? (If you are angry, it may require questioning if you were triggered by something. If unsure, anger may indicate an unmet need, such as setting healthy boundaries or processing events with a friend or therapist. Is this an emotion that can get out of control or an emotion you avoid? Could this be related to mood, grief, betrayal, hunger, overworking, lack of sleep…?) Lonely? Who can I connect to that would be supportive (friend, family, therapist, support group)? Be honest with yourself. Is it challenging to be alone, and if so, what support is needed to be at peace when alone? Are there unprocessed fears or insecurities to work through? How can you add more connection in your life... (church, hobbies, sports, travel, vacation, friend dates, dating, creating a book club, or other activity you enjoy)? Have you tried joining meet-up groups with people with similar interests? Tired? (Checking in with yourself... Are you staying up too late and having issues with sleep? You may need support from a professional or a change in schedule as your mood is hindered by lack of sleep and can cause other health issues and increase stress and reactivity.) As we become adults and take responsibility for improving our self-care, we become better friends, spouses, parents, bosses, and co-workers. We stop projecting our stress toward others and work on containment and respecting our own needs first so that we can show up and be of service. .

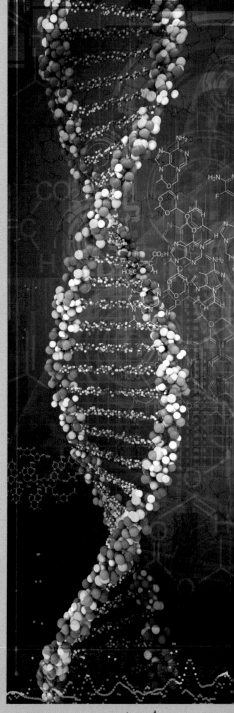

"You must be the change you wish to see in the world" - Gandhi

Take a moment to reflect on what you need right now and practice showing up for yourself by providing whatever you need, such as a nap, a drink of water, food, exercise, or a deep, relaxing breath. I love to put an affirmation on a card to motivate positive thoughts and feelings. I keep them at home, at work, and in my car to pull them out whenever I need a boost from the universe. Be the change you wish to see in the world by being more self-compassionate and practicing practical self-care methods daily.

Playbook Activity:
Meeting needs:

What can you do to support yourself on days where you are tired:

What can you do to support yourself on days where you are lonely:

What can you do to support yourself on days where you are angry:

It is Human to Error... Be relatable by admitting mistakes... Being perfect is impossible!

Perfectionism is a problem and is connected to trauma. The subconscious negative message for Perfectionists is typical, "I am not good enough." This is why perfectionists will kill themselves trying to prove to the world, "Look, I am good enough." They will work overtime, trying to get raises at work, awards, and acceptance, seeking approval so they can think for a moment, "I am enough," but the moment doesn't last. The cycle continues as the perfectionist is intrinsically motivated by the negative subconscious messages to keep proving themselves to get outside validation, which is fleeting. The cup is never full for long. Perfectionists will notice everyone else's mistakes and often go out of their way to point them out. This is subconsciously motivated by their inner fears of making mistakes and not feeling good enough. The perfectionist may continue in this pattern, like a hamster in a wheel until they hit a point of burnout, by constantly overachieving to prove to the world that they are enough! When perfectionists finally overwork themselves until burnout, the shame spiral starts. The shame spiral is when the brain makes the association back to the underlying belief that they are "not good enough," and then the inner perfectionist judge comes out and criticizes with the same old negative belief. The brain likes to be right, so it is constantly seeking evidence that it is, in fact, right. That is why when a negative belief is running the show, such as "I am not good enough," the brain will magnify any mistake. The brain or inner critic will start screaming, "See, there it is again. I will never be good enough!" This can feel like an endless cycle until the perfectionist starts to address the negative core belief and the traumas that contributed to it. By addressing the underlying negative beliefs and healing the trauma, a person can start the road to believing they are indeed enough, and life becomes much easier since they are no longer trying to get constant outside validation. A recovering perfectionist celebrates mistakes and learns to laugh at the old crazy-making cycle while stepping into a more peaceful existence. As a recovering perfectionist, I know I am taking risks when I make mistakes and that I will learn and grow in the process. It is uncomfortable, and I have learned to apologize and have grace with myself. Trying to be perfect is an illusion and a recipe for failure. Life becomes much easier and more relatable when we are authentic. We learn how to laugh at ourselves and celebrate our mistakes. Our mistakes mean we were brave, we can learn something, and move on without the inner critic's voice sending us down a shame spiral of negative thinking.
View life with wonder, open to new adventures.
Adventures either forgotten
or adventures not yet dreamed.
Let yourself imagine
and with this new mind...Dream! - Ria Flanagan

Book Suggestion: Gifts of Imperfection - by Brene Brown

Have fun! Color outside the lines!
Be playful and messy, make mistakes,
and do it with joy and passion...

Week 1

Week 2

Week 3

Week 4

Week 5

You Are the One.... You Have Been Seeking!!

Until we learn how to treat ourselves right, how can we expect anyone else to? If we have been so worried about taking care of everyone else, we may have a long history of neglecting our own wants and needs. This is often due to a history of trauma where we only got our needs met or were validated when we took care of others. We may even struggle with identifying what our wants and needs are because we are not used to having those needs met. If this sounds familiar, I encourage you to make it your mission to figure out what it is that you want and need and start with fulfilling those needs on your own.

Try taking yourself out on the perfect date, which could mean buying yourself your favorite flowers, going to your favorite sports game or movie, ordering the food you want, or taking yourself to your favorite vacation destination (bring a lover or a friend if you wish), but make sure your intention is to fall in love with you and all the miracles around you. Take some time to build the life you want so that adding another human being to it would become an addition or gift, not a need. If we are looking for another person to make us happy, we will always end up being disappointed because happiness is an inside job! Whatever it takes to start living the life that brings you joy, you are responsible for making that happen.

Check out the documentary: www.thehappymovie.com This documentary explores what brings people long-term happiness from a positive psychology perspective, researching countries all over the world. It may surprise you! Watch the film, and after, write down the things that actually bring you joy long-term... You may be surprised that it has little to do with monetary value or things. Once you identify what brings you joy, it may be time to reevaluate your priorities.

Must watch:You are the one you have been looking for By Adam Roa on YouTube: https://www.youtube.com/watch?v=nt5_3cbo31l (Adam Roa, 2017).

Book Suggestion: "Think Like a Monk" by Jay Shetty.

Playbook Activity:
I can take myself out on the best date today!

Brainstorm the best date you could treat yourself to today:

(Best morning coffee, pick myself up my favorite flowers,
take myself to a movie ...) What does it look like:

What did you do? How could you make it even more joyful?

Protect your environment

Reduce toxins, limiting beliefs, and entanglements

It is time to remove the clutter, including toxic cleaning chemicals, remove dust, and donate old clothes and items that no longer bring you joy (Kondō, 2014). Learn about harmful additives in food, and consider nourishing your body with foods that provide sustainable energy instead of spiking blood sugar and crashing soon after eating them. Clear out the clutter in your food, home, and social life. We are impacted by our environment, the friends we keep, the foods we eat, and the beliefs we hold onto that no longer serve us. We leave a footprint on this earth, and we can make responsible choices about the brands we support and our purchases; even when it seems like the change is small, when we are all making small changes together, it can create an impact like a tidal wave. Your body is the environment that you live in, your home away from home. Have you thanked your body today? Showed gratitude by providing it the necessary nourishment and love to support you. I know that I did not appreciate my body in my twenties when I was in great shame and had all the energy in the world, sadly! But it is not too late to appreciate it now. I know it can be complicated with all the marketing and advertising brainwashing us to think we must look a certain way, but how boring would it be if we all looked the same? Besides, all those images are photoshopped anyway. We are all uniquely gorgeous! Listen to YouTube video, Reshape your Mind, Not Your Body by Bridgette Ugarte: https://www.youtube.com/watch?v=Jr4zxhI1FVg Listening to affirmations before sleep can help to rewire the subconscious brain. As we learn to care for ourselves, we model self-love for future generations. Change and happiness start from within and have a ripple effect. Integrate movement, breath, and affirmations as a morning stretching routine to motivate yourself and get your blood circulating. Create a music set that makes you want to get up and move. Be creative, and be gentle with your exercise routines, as we only have one body. Just enjoy the life you have left and protect your environment and body! How do the people in your life inspire you? If they do not bring you joy, it may be time to create some space to identify what they are doing in your environment. What is the price you pay to keep them there?

Start a list on your phone, paper, or white board of what you want to remove from your environment today to improve health and mental clarity!

Playbook Activity:
Supportive or harmful?

Check-in to assess if people and things in your life are supportive or potentially harmful. (Do you trust people that are not good for you?) Write out the people you spend the most time with, what activities you do together, and how you feel after spending time with them:

Are there any activities or people you want to reduce time spent or eliminate from your life?

How can you change your mind about your body to feel love for yourself right now in this moment?

Mind-Body Connection

"EVERY THOUGHT WE THINK IS CREATING OUR FUTURE." Louise Hay

Attuning to health and wellness is being connected to self in mind and body. Ask yourself: to optimize my health, what changes do I need to make? Is it changes in diet, meeting with a nutritionist, joining a gym and consulting with a trainer to guide me in the right direction, or learning what exercise is best to reduce injuries (learning our limits)? If running is causing stress to your body, maybe it is time to trying new things. Health options below:

- Yoga Tai Chi
- Community sports team
- Zumba
- Martial Arts
- Spin class
- Belly Dancing
- Core strength training
- Karate
- Pilates
- Meditation (guided meditations are a good way to start this process)
- Acupuncture
- Regular Massage

You can work with a doctor to find out if your hormone levels are balanced, and take blood tests to make sure you are healthy and not vitamin-deficient. Get regular check-ups with your doctor to support you living your best life. A mindset of being preventative rather than waiting for a problem to happen can be game changing. Are you eating foods that create bloating and discomfort, negative moods, or allergic reactions? Have you learned about the dangers of having a diet heavy in processed foods or high in sugar?

Working with specialists to create a healthy, balanced diet is critical to living your best life. In yoga, they say perfect breath is perfect health. Take several moments throughout your day to practice full breaths and slow the mind. Close your eyes and picture the visual workshop you created at the beginning of this course. Take a seat, and for a few minutes, close your eyes and breathe, look up at your screen in your workspace, and ask the question, "What do I need to do or add to my life to be in my best health?" Notice what comes up? Write it down and start creating a list of goals to help balance your mind and body. Add something to your routine that improves the quality of your life. You are worth it! If you have unresolved trauma, work with a trauma therapist to resolve it, or it will impact your health over time. It is so vital to release resentments and process forgiveness for your own health. Carrying old wounds is taxing on the nervous system and is an unnecessary weight slowing you down. If you find yourself being reactive to things or perseverating on bad memories, you may have unresolved trauma triggers, and reaching out to a trauma-trained counselor would be an excellent first step. Dr. Gabor Mate and Dr. Peter Levine speak about all of us having trauma. Just turning on the news can remind you that we do not live in a world where there is peace on earth, but there are methods to create more peace in our nervous systems. Book suggestion: "You Can Heal Your Life" by Louise Hay. I love the affirmations in the middle of the book that connect to physical issues in the body. I have personally found the affirmations helpful and accurate.

Playbook Activity:

Breathing in affirmations while stretching and breathing out negativity is a great practice while warming up for a workout. The affirmations go deeper into your subconscious as you connect your mind, body, and breath. Remember to use "I am" statements. Breathe in "I am enough," and breathe out thoughts that do not serve your highest self.

Try some meditations on YouTube or apps with guided meditations.

App Suggestion: Ekhart Yoga. What grounding activities
can you add to your day today to reduce stress?

Mind Body Connection Conntinued......

When we are not taking the time needed to rest, we are more susceptible to nervous system dysregulation, which can be harmful to our health if this occurs for long periods of time. In a culture that values hard work, we also have high rates of heart attacks and autoimmune issues. In his book 'The Myth of Normal,' Dr. Gabor Mate discusses correlations between female caregivers and developing autoimmune issues (Gabor, 2022). We can become triggered by something that reminds us of past unresolved trauma, and we can enter a fight-flight or freeze state, which is different than having emotions. These states are connected to survival (the autonomic nervous system). Fight and flight reactions can be helpful when trying to run from or fight off an attacker but are not beneficial reactions in our daily lives when responding to our bosses, partners, family members, or children. If this happens, it is best to rest and then consult with a therapist who has experience with treating trauma.

Book suggestion: Thrive: The Third Metric to Redefining Success and Creating a Life of Well-Being, Wisdom, and Wonder – Arianna Huffington

Eye movement desensitization reprocessing (EMDR) (Emdr Basic Training, 2024) and somatic experiencing (SE) (Somatic Experiencing International [SEI], 2024) are a couple of trauma modalities that are highly effective in treating trauma reactions.

Finding an experienced therapist that you connect with is equally important. One way to determine that you are having a trauma reaction is that your response is not proportionate to the situation. This may be taking you a long time to calm down, and when you do, you feel drained. Have you heard the saying, "If we are hysterical, it is historical?" This refers to being triggered by some unresolved past trauma. Doing a trauma timeline with a therapist can also help to locate potential memories that can be processed in therapy. It is essential to integrate a process that incorporates breath and movement because trauma is stored in the body. Spending time in nature is an excellent way to start grounding and connecting the brain and body.

Book suggestion about how trauma is stored in our bodies:
The Body Keeps the Score - By Bessel Van der Kolk

Playbook Activity:
Brainstorm a list of ways you can increase your mind-body connection... Next, add one thing to this week's schedule!

Week 2: Is there something you desire to change about your schedule?

Week 3: Add Something to your routine you have always wanted to try. What is it?

Week 4: What is working and what isn't? Make desired changes, this is your life!

The Universe Has
YOUR BACK

Are you spiritual or religious? Do you relate more to science? Do you believe in a power greater than yourself? This greater power could be science, the ocean, God of a specific religion, oxygen, the ocean, nature, or a door handle (entering a new environment, dimension, immediate mindfulness as you look forward). I have heard others say it's their 12-step community, family, the emotion of love. What is your higher power right now? I challenge you to be honest with yourself; if you have one, are you in loving connection to it? If you don't have one, is it possible that you have placed a person in this role, a substance or material object, or your work as your higher power? This typically doesn't end well. Look closely at your life, and if needed, make changes that are more supportive of having balance. A good way to check in with yourself is by journaling your goals and noticing if you validate yourself with outside things, which can include material items (car, house, job, power, money, partner), your identity being based on the outside, using relationships to affirm yourself or people, or pay checks. The problem is that all those people and things can go away, and then what?

What is important to notice throughout history and all over the world is that there has always been a spiritual world in whatever form (cave paintings to Egyptian tombs). What is important for all of us is to feel supported and connected to one another and the world we live in. Our actions affect others, and when you live from a mindset of, "The universe has my back," you feel supported, and it helps let go of being in a state of feeling like you always have to control everything or prove yourself. I mean, let's be honest, we really have very little that we can control. We definitely lose when trying to control others. When we open up to our intuition, an inner knowing, and we connect to something bigger than ourselves, it is a weight lifted. We don't have to be in a state of constant worry, as this literally only causes more stress. My encouragement is to plan as normal, let go of the rest, take a breath, and relax when someone cancels. Let go with love instead of fear. The universe has your back if you would just receive the messages and support that is all around you. Asking for help is key to this process, and receiving it is part of allowing someone to give you a gift. Remember, you do not have to carry the weight of the world on your back because it ultimately is not up to you anyway.

Playbook Activity:

Letting go:
1) Take a deep breath, hold your hands up, and squeeze them tightly into fists.
2) Visualize trying to control something that is not working
while holding your breath for a count of four
3) Next, open your palms up while releasing your breath.
4) Notice the lightness as you exhale and let the tension leave
5) Visualize the thing you were trying to control working out effortlessly

The universe has your back. Trust that you are supported, and look
for the doors opening around you. Notice how it feels in your body
to let go... and enjoy the weightlessness for a moment.

Listening to Your Intuition

Intuition is essential to helping make decisions and answer internal questions. To do that, accessing and connecting to your emotions is vital. Learn to tolerate emotions, expand your tolerance window, and gain the wisdom that comes from them. Suppose you have been numbing your feelings with substances, Netflix, work, business, gambling, sex, or relationships. In that case, getting help with letting go of this pattern is crucial to becoming proficient in accessing your emotions.

Our intuition is essential in making major life decisions that no one else can make for us. You can help get in touch with intuition by journaling, therapy, talking to friends, silent time, art therapy, and meditation. These are great ways to process decisions as you connect deeper to your intuition. There are many times when the answer is not apparent, and this is when intuition is critical. Spending time in silence to connect to your emotions while sitting with the questions you have can be helpful. Take a few minutes to enter your creation station you created at the beginning of the playbook. Once you have entered your creation station, sit down and look at the screen you set up to see if you can connect to some guidance. You can visualize calling out to some wise masters to help you navigate this decision and allow yourself to be open to receiving. You could create a time machine in your creation station to see the future or speak to someone you trust. Allow this creative process to open doors that logic and reason may not see.

If you are stressed, it may help to meditate, exercise, and take some deep breaths to relax before doing this so you are more open to creativity and guidance. When we are connected to our intuition, it has a similar feeling when we know something to be true. It feels true. Think about how you can feel someone is lying, even if they are a good liar. It is a different feeling when you know something to be accurate, an inner knowing. Intuition is connected to this inner knowing. We all have this ability, but it helps to actively tune into it daily, like building muscle; it takes practice. After having children, my intuition was enhanced in ways I never imagined. I can sense my toddler is up to trouble even when it is silent, sneaky trouble. A great book related to intuition is by Gavin de Becker, titled "The Gift of Fear."

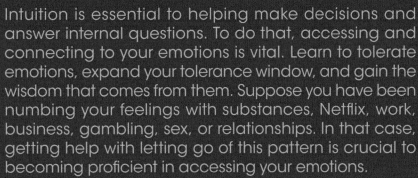

"PROGRESS, NOT PERFECTION, IS WHAT WE SHOULD BE ASKING OF OURSELVES." *Julia Cameron*

Playbook Activity:
Take a minute to write down a couple of times that you were connected to your intuition to reflect on what was going on at the time. Fear can rise up to try and protect you. Do you remember a time when fear saved you?

Open up to the Miracles!

"Where are the miracles?"

I had no idea how to answer a client when asked in the middle of a group I was running, "Where are the miracles?" I listened to my intuition, and some words blurted out my mouth: "Miracles are everywhere. When you are open to seeing them, miracles are everywhere." I appeared confident when speaking those words, only because my intuition was clear. Later, I worried that the client would come to the group the next day and tell me I was full of it! I am thankful that my intuition spoke up that day because when the client returned to the group, she shared how making a shift in her perception changed everything. As soon

as her perspective changed, she was witnessing miracles everywhere.

Joining a support group, coaching group, or recovery group can help elevate and inspire members to make changes at an accelerated rate. Passion, joy and love have a ripple effect.

This was a powerful reminder that when we shift our perspective and become open to all that is miraculous in the world, it is undeniable that miracles are right in front of us. Walk through nature and notice all that is alive around you. Look within and see all the amazing things your body does for you that you do not need to think about! Focus on remaining open to all the miracles; they will suddenly be everywhere. When we look for what works in the world and our lives, we change our perspective and become amazed at everything we have been blind to.

You get more of what you focus on. Stop the worry habit! Start a manifestation habit!

Sometimes, it may seem that things are going wrong, like that day you spilled something on your shirt and had to change clothes, and then you arrived late for work. It can seem like things are not going right, but what if you believed that the universe has your back and switched your perspective? Possibly, you were saved from a possible car accident by being a few minutes behind schedule. Picture your favorite person wishing you safety and joy; now, picture this wish as a ball of colorful energy draped around you, protecting you. Instead of worrying about someone, send them well wishes or visualize sending a cloak of protective, loving energy. This is similar to the power of prayer, which has an energy like radio waves. If the word prayer is uncomfortable, try the reframe of sending energy. Worrying only creates more worry and creates dysregulation in the nervous system. This helps no one ever.

Playbook Activity:
Notice everyday miracles (ex. "I woke up today") and brainstorm
ways to help you stay focused on what is going right in your life.
Practice an energy cloak visualization today on someone you worry
about and throw out the worry habit. Track progress below:

Embracing EMOTIONS

Start to think of your emotions as guides.

As you learn how to tolerate your emotions, you can start to change your mindset and embrace them. Emotion leads you into healing, creating healthy boundaries, gaining awareness, abundance, energy, and spirituality, and clarity on how to clearly communicate your wants and needs. Think about when you were growing up. Who did not support you in having your emotions, and when did you start to shut them off? Now is the time to embrace emotions and find the gifts they are trying to communicate. You can start by using your breath as a gate of permission, allowing yourself to notice where sensations show up in the body as you breathe. Anger can feel like energy or tension all over your body. Fear can feel like tightness in the upper chest, suffocation, or a sensation in your stomach. Passion is a sustainable energy force-feeding creativity and excitement. Start to notice how emotions affect your body, and then fill the body with breath, slowly breathing in through the nose and out through your mouth. Continue a few deep breaths until the emotion passes through like a wave. In the process, notice if there is an image, belief, memory, or additional sensation that needs attention paid to it. Practice being present for yourself while nurturing through this process. You may want to be in your creation station and visualize angels/guides/beloved family members supporting you through your growth. You are re-parenting yourself by allowing yourself to feel and gain wisdom from your emotions. Meditation can help grow awareness around emotions. Meditation can help support your intuition by calming the overactive mind, so we can easily shift into breathing through the emotions instead of falling into the old subconscious habit of stuffing them.

Have you ever heard of an AFGO? It means, "Another Fucking Growth Opportunity!" Sorry for the swear word, but this acronym helps me remember the gift of feeling pain, which is growth. When I am experiencing uncomfortable growth, feeling pain, and other emotions that pop up, I remind myself that I am learning lessons to mature and gain the wisdom I need to move forward. Often, when we feel stuck, it can be because we are numbing out our emotions (this can be with drugs, alcohol, spending, gambling, pornography, video games, sex, using relationships, and caretaking others...). When we are numb, we cannot gain the gifts all the emotions have to bring into our lives. There are many reasons we could be suppressing our emotions; maybe we had parents who modeled suppressed feelings or were told the emotion was unacceptable in multiple ways growing up, through school or daycare, peers, or lovers. What emotions were encouraged when you were growing up, and which emotions were usually punished? Can you identify the gifts of each emotion and start allowing the emotions to be your guides? Now is the time to practice feeling your feelings, removing judgment, and letting them bring essential gifts to your life. Can you separate healthy anger from sideways anger or rage? Intensive workshops can help release past trauma still stored in the body. Workshops run by licensed professionals at Rio Retreat: https://www.themeadows.com/workshops/ Workshops at Onsite: https://experienceonsite. com/workshops/ Empowerment workshops with me: https://iwsuccessworkshops.com/ Books to explore: "Anger" by Thich Nhat Hanh

Releasing EMOTIONS

Move out suffering create space for joy

Playbook tip: Allow room for all the emotions, with the knowledge that each one has a gift for you to aid in maturity and development. You are at risk of arrested development if you are numbing out emotions. As an adult, acting like a 6-year-old or teenager is a sign of unresolved trauma and arrested development. The more you practice feeling the feelings, the easier it is, and rapid growth will occur. Take a deep breath, fill up your chest and belly, and visualize oxygen flowing all the way down to your toes. Next, slowly exhale. Ask yourself, "What am I feeling?" and write down where the sensation is in your body. Feeling emotions takes place in the body, not in the mind. You are integrating the mind and body as you track where the feelings are connected to your body. Awesome work! You got this! I use Pia Mellody's 8 Basic Emotions chart in my office with my clients. I have it printed on large boards to help clients identify where the sensations are in the body when feeling the emotions, here is a link from the Claudia Black Young Adult Center website: https://www.claudiablackcenter.com/all-of-the-feels-accepting-the-gifts-of-emotion/ I like Pia Mellodys' chart because it helps clients locate and name the emotion and connect to the gifts of each emotion, which is motivational to allow one to feel the feelings instead of blocking them out. Fear is often in the upper chest, with sensations of tightness and suffocation. Mellody, 2024). If you gave fear a color, what would it be? I love the Pixar movie Inside Out, where each emotion has a character (Docter & Del Carmen, 2015). As you write about your feelings, you could create a character for each to be playful as you grow and increase your emotional intelligence. Check out the therapeutic model below if you are interested in learning more about how trauma stunts maturity. Suggested therapy model: The Meadows Model created by Pia Mellody at website: https://meadowsbh.com/the-meadows-model/

In the Somatic Experiencing training, a trauma modality created by doctor Peter Levine I attended, we practiced a lot of expansion and pendulation of emotions to work with our clients (SEI, 2024). One of my favorites was magnifying joy by picking a favorite experience, pet, or image (ice cream, puppy, kitten, sunset in Hawaii) and allowing yourself to sit with it and breathe into it until it expands throughout your body. This is a playful, fun practice I suggest implementing daily to expand your window of tolerance to feel and receive more joy in your life! Watch it grow and track progress. When we have become accustomed to numbing our emotions or suffering from trauma, we may need to practice sitting in happiness. Start your day with this happiness-inducing daily practice! I understand that allowing yourself to access and feel your feelings may be uncomfortable, especially if you have been stuffing, numbing, or running from them. Most humans use numbing out in some way (binge-watching Netflix or overworking). It could be like confronting a dragon locked up in a faraway dark dungeon long ago, and why would you want to allow that creature out in the world? Having a licensed professional guide you in the early stages is beneficial, mainly when unresolved trauma is in the body. The truth is that healing is in the feeling, and stuffing emotions only creates a dragon with more fire to exhale, which eventually comes out sideways (Examples: depression, anxiety, rage, suicidal ideation, overeating, starving self, acting out behaviors, addiction, health issues, perfectionism, obsession). Once you are in a regular cycle of feeling your feelings, using your breathing to move them through your body with ease, and allowing the gifts and wisdom they have for you, it becomes like riding a wave. I recently attended BASE training with Dave Berger, my original (OG) Somatic Experiencing instructor. I experienced deep emotional release when receiving this sensing work from licensed professionals. Check out the BASE website: https://daveberger.net/base If you want to learn more. Combining psychology with professionals' sensing/somatic work is the future for positive changes in healthcare in my experience.

Playbook Activity
Take an inventory of the messages you received from your childhood about each emotion (Anger, Fear, Pain, Joy, Passion, Love, Shame, and Guilt)? Which emotions do you express most in your life? Which emotions do you typically try to suppress or avoid feeling?

Start a new habit of connecting to and writing down the feeling you had each day (breath, sense into the body with your breath) What am I feeling?

Was there a gift or lesson this emotion was communicating?

Is there a limiting belief connected to trauma I want to change, seek support, process and let go of?

If a negative cognition or limiting belief is present what process can I begin to move this out (affirmations (500 day), therapy, coaching, support group, workshop, course, mindfulness...)?

Workbook suggestion: Mind Over Mood: Change How You Feel by Changing the Way You Think (Greenberger et al., 2015)

Boundaries Protect our Joy

It would be helpful if we could physically see boundaries, so I suggest always visualizing a boundary around you. I love reminding myself that "what other people think about me is not my business." Other people's opinions are really about them, not you. How amazing would your life be if you stopped personalizing other people's realities and prioritized your inner peace? Start by mindfully visualizing a boundary around you; you could visualize a bubble, an impenetrable protective barrier, that you can see and hear through. In certain situations, like with a demanding boss or confrontational person, you may need to visualize a protective layer of armor, a magic cloak, or a ring of fire, to protect you from other people's opinions, judgments, and criticisms. Think about it: the most critical people are typically unhappy with themselves and unconsciously project negativity onto everyone else. I also love the saying, "It is not my circus, and they are not my monkeys." When I say this, I extend my arms in a circle around me to indicate my boundary. I consciously choose not to let other people's chaos disrupt my peace. Taking on the opinions and emotions of others is a way of abandoning one's self. It can be helpful to consult with experts on many topics, but taking on others' opinions without boundaries can be harmful because it does not allow you to make a factual assessment, which helps when making an informed opinion. It can be beneficial to pray for support when the facts are insufficient, or if prayer is not in your wheelhouse, use visualization. Close your eyes and visualize a white light wrapped around your boundary, helping you not pick up other people's emotional baggage. It only works if you try this, not just intellectualize it, walk through the process, and notice how it feels in your body with the knowledge that the universe wants you to be safe and protected. Take a deep breath and use your hands to feel the space between your body and the edge of your boundary, notice the sensations of feeling protected and having the space to formulate your own opinions and feel only your emotions. This will provide you with the space and time you need for clarity to develop. Judgment is never helpful, be it towards ourselves or others. Taking on another's reality, emotions, criticisms, or judgments doesn't help them or you and can be confusing. I will visualize my boundary protecting me from all that energetic chaos, send back any energy (emotions and opinions) that are not my own, and say to myself, "Please take back anything I am carrying that is not mine. Please send it back to whomever it came from so they can learn their lessons, and I take back anything that was mine so I can learn my lessons." I had an acupuncturist share this with me, and I love using it to help clear away other people's energy (emotions, judgments, and opinions). When we caretake others all the time, we may be using this method of coping to avoid our own emotions or issues. Caretaking may become a distraction from our true purpose. When this happens, you may feel exhausted, and caretaking could affect your health and growth. If you feel defeated or angry, thinking, "I am always there for others, and no one is here for me," you may need to re-evaluate your boundaries. When we practice healthy boundaries, we improve our self-care. You will do a better job of helping others without depleting yourself, which is the catalyst for harboring resentment. We all have a certain amount of energy to get through the day, so it is crucial, to be honest with yourself about how much energy you have for others and how much you need to stay mentally and physically healthy for yourself. When you overextend yourself, you burn out and are abandoning your own wants and needs. You are not having boundaries. It is perfectly fine to say, "I can't help today, maybe tomorrow."

Playbook Activity:

Do a mental inventory of everyone in your life, and notice if you feel there is a healthy exchange of energy or if you feel weighed down by some of your relationships. Of course, everyone has ups and downs, and we want to be supportive, but I am talking more about people who may be taking more than they are giving energetically all the time. How can you shift your boundaries to protect your mental and emotional health in these relationships?

Examples: Spend less or no time with people that only talk about themselves. Spend more time with people you feel empowered and inspired with. Write below some changes you can make to support you being in your best self:

"FORGIVENESS IS THE GREATEST GIFT WE CAN GIVE OURSELVES."

Maya Angelou

Carrying a grudge only hurts you and holds you back from growth and freedom.

Try different ways to process out old resentments or hurt so you can lighten your load in life. I am not saying what other people did to you was not horrible, it may have been, but it is about them, not you. Take your power back by holding a strong boundary to not let them hurt you again, but also, process the hurt out so you can move on and not be attached to this person anymore or carry the weight of the past. Visualize yourself floating in space; imagine a white light surrounding you and protecting you. Now visualize the person you are working on forgiving in a bubble, also surrounded by white light. You can place them at a comfortable distance from you. Now notice blue rays of light that are connecting the two of you. Notice where the light is on your body, and slowly gently pick up the light cord from your body and release it. If there are more cords, just one by one, pick them off you (like removing lint from your jacket) and release them into space. Visualize the white light washing over you once all the blue cords are gone. Slowly breathing in and out with deep breaths, watch as the person drifts away from you. You are safe, healed, and protected.

It can even be helpful to do this visualization with friends and family members that you are still close to. Notice how relationships change as you let go of the past and move forward without resentments. Working on forgiveness in therapy is an effective way to process through forgiveness, sharing with friends, reading books on the process of forgiveness, journaling, and actively making a choice to process the feelings and move on. A wonderful Hawaiian practice about forgiveness of self and others called, ho'oponopono, translates roughly to return to balance or source (love) and includes mantras or prayers. This one was shared with me years ago while visiting Sedona: I am sorry. Please forgive me. Thank you. I love you. I am amazed at what I release every time I say this. Resentments I never knew I had rose to the surface, and then I feel lighter. No need to hang on to anger or pain, but know you can protect yourself from being hurt again, and follow up with using appropriate boundaries. Morrnah Nalamaku Simeona is the founder of the modern practice of Ho'oponopono which she has practical applications on. You can learn more on this website: https://hooponoponomiracle.com/ho-oponopono-technique/ She was named "the living Treasure of Hawaii" in 1982 j(Ho'oponopono Technique - How to Practice the Hawaiian Self Healing Process, 2020).

Playbook Activity:
Forgiveness

1)Write out the name of a person you are ready to forgive:

2) Write the name of a person you are not ready to forgive:

3) Write one thing you want to forgive yourself for:

4) Write about how you felt different when you were forgiven or you forgave someone:

5) Take a breath and reflect on your writing. Any insights?

Suggestion: Repeat the ho'oponopono mantra 3 times with deep breaths in between and make note of any shifts emotionally.
"I am sorry
Please Forgive me
Thank you
I love you."

Addressing CHILDHOOD WOUNDS

When someone experiences developmental trauma or childhood trauma, such as a break from a significant attachment figure, they can experience regression as an adult. This could be due to divorce, domestic violence in the home, a sibling with special needs, a parent who was often away due to work, caregivers with mental illness, PTSD, or addiction. If you ever feel like you are being abandoned as an adult or have feelings of powerlessness in relationships or life situations, this indicates a younger self or possible regression happening that links to childhood trauma. It is the wounded child who had no choice, or maybe the defensive teenager (jumping to defensive anger or rage easily) that is driving the car of your life. It is important to ground yourself by taking a few deep breaths and asking yourself, "What could the adult version of myself do instead? What must I do to feel empowered and be the best version of my adult self."

As an adult, you cannot be abandoned, you are not powerless, and you have a choice. You may have feelings of abandonment and powerlessness, which indicates a possible regression to a very young age when you may have been abandoned, powerless, and did not have a choice. Identifying this is happening is the first step to getting the support you need. It may be through a coach, therapist, or workshop to heal developmental trauma, but the choice is now yours, and know you can heal. It can be helpful to read books about healing childhood trauma and learn how trauma interrupts the developmental process and can create feelings of regression.

I walk clients through inner child visualization, empowering them to rescue their wounded child or angry teenager and learn how to nurture and affirm parts of self still suffering. This often includes physical movements of rocking back and forth (use a rocking chair if available) while holding a teddy bear or pillow to represent the younger self. Practice making eye contact with your wounded child (picture yourself between ages 3 and 6); you could use an old photo of yourself to help. Use affirmations to validate and protect your younger self. You begin the journey to healing developmental wounds by using affirmations with touch (place your hand on your heart). It is essential to work with a therapist to process any trauma memories, but practicing daily nurturing and affirming of the self can be done at home.

I suggest doing this first thing in the morning or before bed, saying several affirmations... Examples that are universal (always use "I" statements to help retrain your brain):

"I am enough."
"I am safe."
"I am loved, lovable, and loving."
"I am worthy."
"I have a choice."
"I am valuable."
"I am important."
"The universe has my back."

If you have trouble believing any of these affirmations, I suggest repeating them throughout your day (out loud when no one is listening or exchanging affirmations with a like-minded friend). If you say 500 affirmations a day for 4 weeks, you will start to create new neurotransmitters in the brain, and you will typically start believing these affirmations to be true, which they are! You can begin to feel better! Why let the B.S. belief systems keep you stuck? Don't take my word for it... Give it a whirl!

Playbook Activity:
The affirmations that will support me in achieving my goals are...

Tip: You are being your most evolved adult self when you are affirming yourself, so start a regular routine (5 minutes in the morning and 5 minutes before bed. Show up for you and practice this until it becomes a habit) Commit to 90 days and assess how you are feeling, and if it is effective keep doing what works!

Say a minimum of 500 affirmations a day (Ex. every door you walk through say the affirmation 5 times, repeat all day or when working out, or getting dressed in the morning)

Book Suggestion: Growing Yourself Back Up: Understanding Emotional Regression - by John Lee

Embracing the inner *REBEL*

We all have the rebellious teenager inside

They come out in different ways, like avoiding responsibility, anger, defiance, rage, shutting down, walling people off, blaming others, arrogance, judging, and self-sabotage. The work to heal and integrate our inner teenager begins with self-compassion and acceptance (and a therapist or coach). That teenager helped us to survive, typically without many tools, trying to define our identity and seeking independence. Embrace this part of yourself, celebrating the survival instincts that kept you alive while taking the keys back to the driver's seat of your life. When we let our inner teenagers drive the car to our lives, we are more susceptible to crashing. Many adults live life more like teenagers than functional adults, including world leaders, celebrities, and sometimes our parents.

Visualize loving and accepting that inner rebel, and then take the car keys of your life back from them.

You can lovingly thank your inner rebel for being such a tough badass and let them go hang out with their friends and have fun instead of running your life. Sometimes, you can tell the teenager has taken over because you are making decisions out of anger. One powerful gift of anger is energy; learning to harness this energy as a functional adult is empowering. Using this energy and transforming it from anger into action can look like setting boundaries, using direct communication, speaking up for yourself respectfully, advocating for your wants and needs, and protecting yourself.

If your reaction feels out of control, going from a zero to ten in seconds, this is another issue entirely, often referred to as a "trauma reaction." It may mean you have some unresolved issues or trauma, and seeking help from a mental health professional is wise. When hurt people do not take responsibility as adults to heal themselves, they will most likely hurt others... "Hurt people, hurt people." The functional adult takes responsibility for these issues and turns to trusted experts for support. Your inner rebel may not have had the tools to heal when you were young, but it is never too late to heal and bring peace to the inner rebel now. We do this by reparenting ourselves through setting healthy limits and having self-compassion through this process. We can be grateful for all that our inner rebels did for us to help us survive. At the same time, we can hold space to make decisions from our functional adult self instead of our reactive, rebellious self. Book suggestions: Facing Codependence by Pia Mellody

Playbook Activity:
Write out times when you may be in your inner rebel:

"I am acting in my inner rebel when I do this or say this..."

1) Is this helpful, or do I need support with this behavior (therapist, coach, trusted friend)?

2) What can I do to hand the keys back of my life back to my adult self so I don't do damage?

3) Is there ever a time when the inner rebel is the truth-teller (trying to express a need or want that is not being met) and is helpful?

4) How can I apply this insight into my adult life (ex., communicate wants and needs directly, ask for help...)?

Book suggestion: No Bad Parts - by Richard Schwartz

Self EMPOWERED

Happiness is being embodied and empowered!

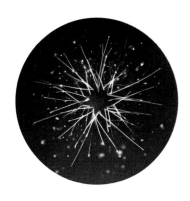

There are many ways to relate to the 'empowered self.' Different terms I have heard, "the highest self" or the "enlightened self," refer to when we are in connection with spirit, intention, God, the universe, humanity, or whatever makes sense to you as a reference, but basically when you are in truth, intention, and feel at peace. Acting from our true selves can feel effortless and blissful when we are in our purpose. For when an artist is creating, a preacher is giving a powerful sermon, or someone chooses life over death, an addict finds the path to recovery, a child is first held by its mother, the earth heals itself, a crime is brought to justice, a truth is revealed or several events that muster feelings of peace. Being true to yourself and living your life purpose is straightforward and blissful, and you feel reenergized even when working all day. Have you ever experienced a feeling of flow in what you were doing at the moment? Many athletes, musicians, and artists share these moments with us in their careers (Csikszentmihalyi, 2022). You can feel these artists were on fire when they were entirely in the moment, and everything looked easy, and it was inspiring to watch. I enjoy watching documentaries where the artists describe these memorable moments of flow in their careers. One of my recent favorites is the musician PINKs documentary, All I Know So Far (Gracey, 2021). Do you have a favorite musician you love to watch play? But what about the average person? We are all capable of being in flow and feeling empowered. Part of what keeps us from these moments of flow in our lives is our self-criticism and living in the past or present. If you are fully present in each moment, doing your best and letting go of judgment is the best way of joining with a flow state. When we trust we are where we need to be, things tend to be less stressful. I enhanced my flow state when working with Amisha Patel in her Evolve Workshop (Patel, 2022). Working with a coach was a supportive, interactive experience, and I recommend researching this option. I walked out of that experience with more flow, courage, and love than when I started! I highly encourage finding communities you thrive in!

Playbook Activity:
Remember a time in your life when things flowed for you, maybe in sports, creative arts, public speaking, writing, debate, helping others, or anything that felt effortless and fulfilling. Brainstorm ways to bring more creative energy into your everyday life. If you love to dance or sing and it brings you joy, add more to your daily living. Consider playing music during daily activities and chores, and add dancing and singing as you work. You can build creative expression into your everyday life and become empowered by being fully present in each moment.

1) A time when things were going really well... What was I doing that was joyful, fun, playful, creative?

2) Ways I can add creativity into everyday living...

Your Past Does Not Define You

Your past does not define you; it was a stepping stone into the now and important to get you to this moment. If you live in the past, the "what if" or the "I should have," then you are lost and not able to create a future that is not tied up in the past. The past cannot be changed and is not where you are now. Get present, take a breath, and let go of what brought you here, only knowing that it was an essential part of your journey. If you were to view your life from a new perspective. Believing that everything you have survived has been integral to creating the amazing person that you are today. That each tragedy has brought essential growth and wisdom to your life and helped you develop resilience, character, and depth. If we could view our challenges as gifts and learn how to celebrate that we are alive right now by giving ourselves this clean slate, we would become free from the chains of our past. Now you can create the future you really want and break patterns that no longer serve you.

Book Suggestion: "The Language of Letting Go" by Melody Beattie

When we are free from the past, it allows us to focus on building our future. Where you allow your thoughts to spend time matters. Choose loving thoughts.

Playbook Activity:
Today, put your past behind you and get curious about where you are and all the support that helped you survive.

Who are the people that inspired you? Supported you? Loved you? Write out what they did that was helpful.

Today, practice loving yourself unconditionally and notice how different that may feel. Experient by thinking, "what would I do differently if I loved myself completely in this situation?"

This will help support you in continuing this as a daily mantra: "I love myself unconditionally in this present moment." Write down what you did differently and any new results...

You Can Create Your Future!

First, we must unlearn the negative beliefs and behaviors influenced by our parents, society, peers, and our ancestors to stop unconsciously repeating mistakes from the past. You can see patterns in families of addiction and abuse that, if not treated, are often replicated subconsciously. When we do not make a conscious, mindful choice to parent differently than we were parented, we will repeat the mistakes done to us. In order to change financial patterns, it is important to reveal your beliefs about success and money. Start by taking an inventory of your historical patterns with money. Do you have trouble saving? Impulse spending? Do you hoard your money and rarely spend it, even on essentials? Next, you want to write down messages you received growing up about money from family, friends, and society. Do you believe that money is dirty? Rich people are rotten? That it is selfish to save money? What do you believe about success? It is important to change these negative messages about money and reframe them into positive messages about money, such as, "Money is abundant in my life," "Having more money means I can help more people," or "Money is just energy, it flows easily through my life. I always have enough."

If you are working on yourself right now, changing your mindset, you are already successful because you are mindfully creating a new road for your life instead of repeating the old broken-down roads of your ancestors. Now is the time to pave the road to your future, be it out of gold if you wish. By taking action over your finances, changing your relationship with money, and learning ways to invest, pay off debt, and gain secondary income if desired. If you need to go buy a lottery ticket to imagine buying your dream house, visualize yourself traveling the world, or creating a non-profit organization to improve the world, then go do it so you can allow your mind to build this future without limits! We often create roadblocks and reasons why we cannot achieve things. We will stop ourselves from following our dreams before we even start. It is important to tap into the creative side of your brain. Spend time visualizing the future you really want; this will help motivate you to start setting weekly goals to move toward this future. Create a vision board and make it big enough to inspire you daily in your room, closet, or workspace. If there is no dream or vision, it is time to create one. This could be taking a journey of researching what really brings passion to the surface for you. When we are living a passionate life where work feels like playtime. You deserve to have an amazing life! Remember that you are already successful; it is now time to follow your passion and create the future you want. Next, we will start learning to live in the present moment and loving ourselves right now. Allowing you to create a new narrative for your future.

Playbook Activity:
List your top 5 accomplishments:

Notice the feelings you have...write them down:

From the emotions of joy, passion, and love, write
out 5 accomplishments you aspire to have to happen
Tip: Always helpful to add a vision board

Learn How to be in the Present Moment

Becoming present is a life-changing, resurrecting, joy-filled, abundant way of being. Being present allows space for miracles, to notice that life, joy, and abundance are all around us. In order to be creative and to visualize, we must learn to be in the now. I encourage everyone on the planet to read Eckhart Tolle's book, "The Power of Now." Start to practice this by observing your own presence. The road to intimacy in relationships is first to become present with the self. When we are distracted by technology, what we have to do that day, constantly multitasking, or numbing ourselves with an addiction, we lose connection to self and others. We are truly alive when we are at peace with the present moment. We are able to tap into our intuition and spirituality and experience passion when we are in the present moment. We grow and become wise when living in the present moment. Truth becomes obvious and we can learn to forgive and release resentments as they are toxins suffocating joy.

As we make a choice to become present, our ability to hear and see others is clear. Our ability to communicate our truth becomes effortless, and the dance of life becomes filled with wonder. Notice as you become present in your life that doing laundry or the dishes can be a meditation to create space for peace and reflection instead of a mundane task. Waiting in a line can become interesting as you observe others around you and tune into all life's mysteries. The present has wisdom, lessons, and gifts for us if we can slow down and just be. Get curious about what is happening now, let go of the past, and trust your future.

Book Suggestion: "The Power of Now" By Eckhart Tolle

As we learn to be more present and increase our ability to see things clearly, we will become more aware of our inner thoughts and how they affect our daily choices and decisions.

Playbook Activity:
Being Present in the moment. Start with sitting quietly in a relaxed stillness with eyes opened or closed for 2 minutes, 120 seconds.

Write down your observations: what did you see/visualize, smell, taste, hear, think, feel, physical sensations?

1) Today or tomorrow try sitting in quiet relaxed stillness for 3 to 4 minutes, and write down your observations? Any changes in your body?

2) Today or tomorrow try sitting in quiet relaxed stillness for 5 or 6 minutes, and write down your observations? Any changes in your body? In your perception?

3) Today or tomorrow try sitting in a quiet, relaxed stillness for 7 to 10 minutes. Write down your observations? Any changes in your body? Changes in your day?

4) Today or tomorrow try sitting in quiet relaxed stillness for 10 to 15minutes. Write down your observations? Any changes in your body? Perception changes? Could you keep practicing this daily and expanding the time?

WHO'S THE BULLY?

How do you speak to yourself? Are you your own best friend, or do you bully yourself? Do you allow other people to talk down to you? Is anyone in your life emotionally, physically, verbally, or sexually abusive to you?

If so, now is the time to stop it and get appropriate support. If you are not feeling safe, it is important to ask for help and guidance on safe steps to protect yourself. If you are your own bully, start to question who modeled this kind of behavior for you. It may help to seek counseling around traumatic childhood experiences or people who contributed to this negative self-talk. It is important to become your own best advocate, your own best friend, and not allow yourself to stay in a life you are not happy with. Having a mentor, therapist, or close friend model being support may be needed to help you learn how to speak differently to yourself. Stand up to anyone who does not support you in living your best life. Let go of old dysfunctional voices in your head that are not supportive of you reaching your goals. You are capable of amazing things, and if you don't believe that, it is time to change how you think about yourself. You are a miracle, you are precious, and you are important to this world. My encouragement is to go out and prove it to yourself. Never let the voice of any bully in your life or your head again! Life is short; enjoy every moment. Only speak to yourself with encouragement and support.

Do not let anyone, even yourself, speak negatively toward you.

No more bullying!

If it happens, which it may, it could be an old habit. It is now time to change this unproductive behavior. Replace any negative self-talk with a supportive statement. Replace "I can't do it" with "I can do it."

Book suggestions: No Bad Parts by Richard Schwartz

Life is short; enjoy every moment.

Playbook Activity:
Write a new dialogue as if you were a supportive coach motivating an athlete. Start a new conversation that is not critical but nurturing, affirmative, and creates feelings of peace and confidence... You got this.

Book Suggestions: You Are a Badass by Jen Sincero

Ditching Belief Systems **that block happiness**

Humans are amazing; we have an innate ability to heal. Many studies using placebo pills have been done, proving in many cases that if someone believes a sugar pill (placebo), is the remedy to their illness they often will start to heal. This is called the placebo effect (Google Dictionary defines it as a beneficial effect produced by a placebo drug or treatment, which cannot be attributed to the properties of the placebo itself and must, therefore, be due to the patient's belief in that treatment). The placebo effect illustrates how powerful our beliefs can be related to our physical and mental health. I want to make note that some of our belief systems, such as "I am not worthy," are complete B.S. (yes, I mean Bullshit!) We are all worthy! Notice that B.S. is also short for Belief Systems. "A belief can be changed, notice beliefs that you may have already changed such as belief in Santa Clause, the Tooth Fairy, and the Easter Bunny…"

When I was studying Anthropology as an undergrad, I remember reading about a tribe that believed if they ever shared the "secret magic" of their tribe with an outsider, they would die. It was reported that, eventually, some secrets were revealed to an anthropologist who was allowed to live with this tribe. The anthropologist studied them while living with them and became very close to the tribe. He became close enough to learn some of the tribe's "secret magic," and it was documented that shortly after the secrets were revealed to the anthropologist, the man who shared these secrets did, in fact, suddenly die. This man was not old or sick before he died. Our belief systems are extremely powerful, and wanting to change them has measurable resistance. It will take a great deal of mindfulness and effort to change negative beliefs, but it can be done. One of the reasons I created a course was to help my clients master the practices to change their negative beliefs. The course inspired this book and can be found at: iwwc.thinkific.com I recently started a podcast for free to help listeners with practices to increase levels of happiness: https://www.youtube.com/@happiness_playbook

Learning about different healing modalities, medicines, faiths, and cultures can be an amazing adventure. If we remain open to healing, it can be beneficial to try new ways of doing this. As we open our minds to new possibilities, it can help to read studies about other people healing their addictions and mental health issues and bringing to life their dreams they formally thought impossible. When we shift our mindset to "anything is possible" and do the footwork, we can notice multiple doors open for us. I had a beautiful, healthy baby girl in my 40s. It was helpful to focus on changing my mindset. Believing I could have a healthy baby was crucial. I also applied many methods of healing to prepare myself, using acupuncture, energetic healing, and therapy and raising my mindset to one that supported my dreams! I did all the recommended blood tests and even hired a Dula for physical and mental support during this process. Having the Dula created a sense of safety for me; she was worth every penny! I encourage you to get as much support as you need to make the changes you want to make in your life.

One way to begin is learning about Eastern medicine which has been around for much longer than Western medicine. I encourage everyone to try Acupuncture, Reiki, Bodytalk, and Craniosacral Therapy and see if it is helpful. I do suggest reading reviews and asking for suggestions from people you trust, as not all practitioners are meant for everyone. One of the modalities I studied and found useful in my own healing is Bodytalk. BodyTalk is an energetic healing modality, created by John Veltheim. Dr. Velteim is a Doctor of Chiropractic and Acupuncture and is a skilled Reiki Master.

I know it does help to try different things and stay with what works for you. Many energetic healing modalities allow for the concept of rapid healing. We are all innately able to heal from within; it is often our old beliefs that keep us stuck.

Try the mantra, "I am healthy now. I am healed," and repeat this often as a reminder to the inner self to activate healing on a conscious level. If this is uncomfortable maybe start with, "I am on the road to healing myself." Sometimes, we need to go deeper to heal unhealthy behavior patterns. If a belief system from childhood feels true even if you know it is not, signing up for an intensive workshop using Post Induction Therapy, created by Pia Mellody. Working with a licensed professional in a workshop can help move out subconscious beliefs with experiential methods. Check out my Empowerment workshop at HYPERLINK "http://www.iwsuccessworkshops.com"www.iwsuccessworkshops.com if you need additional support.

Make an inventory of all the beliefs you inherited growing up from family, peers, and society. Now, think about beliefs you have changed due to life experience, education, or culture. Witness that beliefs can be changed, and change the ones that do not support you having your best life!

1) List a few beliefs you have about yourself that are not supportive:

2) List a replacement belief that would support you for each:

3) Practice the new belief daily and live "as if" you believe the supportive belief to be true. What would you change today?

Hypnosis

Today, it is important to reiterate yesterday's message that holding the belief that "healing is possible" is where healing begins. When we are stuck in an unproductive pattern, stepping outside ourselves for a moment and reflecting on when this pattern started can be helpful. When we notice a destructive pattern, we can reach for the tools to break free. Dr. Patrick Carnes' book, The Betrayal Bond: breaking free of exploitative relationships, is a powerful book that relates how our past trauma can influence our present behaviors and relationships. There is a useful assessment in the book that reviews different ways trauma can create maladaptive behavior patterns in our behaviors and relationships. Trauma bonding is very common for people with abandonment or enmeshment patterns with caregivers, and it can attract us to people in our lives now who replicate patterns of trauma from our past. Many therapies and different modalities can help break unhealthy behavioral patterns. Hypnotherapy is used by some practitioners to help people quit smoking and curb other behaviors and maladaptive patterns. I would encourage you to use a licensed professional instead of someone who just took a course on hypnotherapy. I had an interesting experience with hypnosis while attending a workshop by Dr. Brian Weiss, a psychiatrist who uses hypnosis in his practice. This particular workshop was about using hypnosis to encounter past life regression to help heal clients. Dr. Brian Weis shared that he experienced one of his clients slip into what appeared to be a past life regression. He shared that the client later permitted him to record sessions and allowed him to publish his past life regressions in a book. In this live Workshop, Dr. Brian Weis took everyone through a past life regression experience. I attended this workshop for a paper for one of my final master's classes and reported on the experience. In my paper, I discussed the experience of having a past life regression in Dr. Weis' workshop, concluding that regardless of whether the regression was real or imagined (placebo effect), I did experience healing. I also remember that it seemed to take 5 minutes, but the experience was close to an hour long. I also enjoy listening to Dr. Weis's audio books on meditation and used them in countless groups and many patients reported real relief from Dr. Weis's meditations.

Book suggestions: Meditations, by Brian L. Weiss, M.D.

Playbook Activity:
Write out some experiences you have had that you consider healing in your life. What was helpful and healing about those experiences?

Defining "LOVE"

Has your version of love been contaminated by an unhealthy family system? Do you struggle with healthy relationships with friends, family, or romantic relationships?

Be honest with yourself about what love looks like in your family and if you look for another person to make you happy. If you have been disappointed in relationships over and over, have unresolved childhood trauma (enmeshment or neglect), feel abandoned by partners or smothered by them, or have a string of toxic relationships, I suggest reading Pia Mellody's "Facing Love Addiction" and Miguel Ruiz's book, "The Mastery of Love." These books can help you open up to the possibility that your concept of "love" may be a contaminated version of love, not love. When you were growing up, was love paired with violence, domination, or fear? Was love contingent on certain circumstances? When we clear out the contaminated version of love, we may have witnessed (domestic violence, verbal, or emotional abuse in relationships) we free ourselves to see love as it truly is. Love is about connection, spirituality, and a powerful life force. Love is healing and warm and without shame. Love is the most powerful and healing of all emotions. Abandonment in childhood can look differently for everyone; the death of a parent, a parent with mental illness, addiction, adoption (separated from a parent at birth), parents with anger management issues, or a parent that was gone all the time due to working. Many therapists ask adults in therapy, "Can an adult be abandoned?" I often get the answer "yes," but technically, an adult cannot be abandoned in a relationship. As adults, we cannot call CPS or 911 if our partner leaves the relationship. We can feel abandoned as an adult, which indicates unresolved childhood trauma. If we have these feelings of abandonment as an adult, they can be resolved in therapy, workshops, or through learning how trauma impacts us and how to process these unresolved emotions. The therapeutic modalities I suggest are; EMDR, PIT, and SE, and there are others. One way to look at past intense relationships is as a soul mate relationship. This type of relationship brings lessons and is not often for life. A life partner may be a different kind of relationship with more balance and longevity. A life partner is not someone you need but someone you choose. We often grow and experience painful breakups before we are ready for a life partner. When we stop looking for others to heal our wounds and start healing them internally with mindful effort and support, we become prepared to meet our life partner.

People can use others in the same way, and they abuse drugs, gamble, work too much, or drink alcohol. If we are dependent on our partners to make us happy, then we are not practicing love; we are trying to use them like a drug.

It feels easy and natural when we align with love, centered on giving and being open to receiving love. There is a natural feeling of flow to living a heart-centered life. By choosing love over intensity, you enter a sensation of flow. When in flow, life becomes easy, and energy is rejuvenated. Intensity may have passion and excitement, but it can damage our nervous system over time in the struggle. Love helps us heal our nervous systems! Choose love, learn the difference, and practice receiving love today.

Love is not pain, betrayal, or abandonment. Love is a connection, peace, warmth, and a powerful source of healing. Start with loving you just as you are! Book Suggestion: Waking the Tiger: Healing Trauma - By Peter A. Levine

Playbook Activity:
It may take time to love ourselves fully, but we can start
living as if we do today! What can you do differently
today to live as if you fully love yourself...

Escape blaming self or others

"WHEN THE EGO DIES THE SOUL AWAKES" *Mahatma Ghandi*

Where is blame intruding in your life:

- Do you hang on to resentments, live in fear, have trust issues, or have self-esteem issues (this can be thinking you are better than or worse than another person)?
- Do you get lost in judgment or comparison, quick to anger, impatient, or project blame onto everyone else?
- Do you always blame yourself and carry others' emotions?
- Do you struggle with untreated mental health or physical issues?
- Do you struggle with asking for help?
- Do you need more purpose?

"Happiness is an inside job" does not mean you are alone in working on yourself; it may mean seeking guidance, leaving a toxic relationship, taking a class or workshop, or setting healthy boundaries. Find a mental health professional you trust, or maybe work with a physical therapist, start reading books on personal development, learn how to manage finances, or see a psychiatrist for medication to help manage difficult emotions. Advocate for what is suitable for you!

Ask for suggestions from experts on how to slay your demons. If you didn't need the support, I imagine you would have already slayed them. We can't all be experts at everything, and getting help is part of being a responsible adult. You can do this!

Activity:

Spend some time arranging your schedule to include self care, be it massage, therapy, exercise, a workshop, taking a class, meditation, 12-step meeting; whatever is helpful to you, you need to schedule it.

Remember, you are important and deserve to have support!!!

Book suggestion for Recovery: "A Hole in the Sidewalk: Recovery Person's Guide to Relapse Prevention" By Claudia Black

Recovery from Trauma and addiction book suggestions by Claudia Black: Undaunted Hope and Unspoken Legacy

Playbook Activity:
Visualize having everything that you want and need. What would you add to your life? Write it out here:

As you visualize having it all (again visualize it), How does it feel to have all your dreams come to fruition? Now expand this feeling if positive (if negative, do another visualization removing things and adding new things (be playful, have fun with it) until positive feelings only). Stay with this expansive, positive sensation as long as you can, and magnify it so extend head to toe. I encourage you to bring this feeling of abundance into the rest of your day and notice what shows up!

Reflect below on how your day was and how long you could keep this sensation of abundance below(practice daily):

Manifestation Mindset

Manifesting can be a mindset; it is enhanced by living in a state of feeling you already have abundance.

Think of it this way: "Like attracts like." When we are in a state of lack and focusing on what isn't working, we tend to get more of what is not working. If we can adjust our thoughts by practicing affirmations and spend real-time during our daily activities being in a state of gratitude. You will start to shift gears into attracting more of what you want.

I remember hearing Dr. Wayne Dyer, a respected coach, discussing how he reframed his mindset when paying bills. He would make a point of being grateful for being in a place to pay his bills instead of feeling he was in a state of lack. This conscious shifting into a state of gratitude changed how he felt when he paid his bills. He started feeling joy and attributed this shift in his thinking to helping him manifest more financial abundance. He gave thanks in his mind to the companies trusting him with their services. He identified a change in mood and no longer felt frustrated while paying bills. We create more of what we want by noticing how much we already have and being in the feelings and sensations that financial security brings. This conscious choice to think differently creates a state of mind that helps create more economic security.

Book Suggestion: You Will Believe It When you See It - By Dr. Wayne Dyer

Think about a time when a boss, mentor, or peer expressed gratitude for your hard work. I can attest to wanting to work harder and do more for these people. Now notice the difference when you are ignored for your efforts or even think about times you are criticized or judged by a boss, peer, spouse, or parent. Do you want to work harder to please, or do you feel resentful and want to shut down? Manifesting energy responds to us when we are in gratitude and noticing all the miracles. Focusing on what isn't working may be a bad habit, maybe even with good intentions or thoughts of trying to problem-solve. Ultimately, by simply taking a moment to acknowledge what is going well and working in your life, you save yourself from all the negative feelings created by focusing on what you lack. This negative focus enhances and attracts more negative feelings and sensations. Gratitude is the formula for manifesting more of what you truly want. You have the choice of what you focus on. You can shift into a gratitude manifestation mindset today!

Playbook Activity:
Creation Station. Visualize your creation station again and
notice if you want to add some new rooms or items.

Write out new rooms or items added:

Build a new space in your creation station you want to be in while you are practicing your expansion activities, and to be in that room, take 5 to 15 minutes for your visualizations that support your feeling empowered to start your day. Write out anything new you are noticing (practice daily):

Reframing Financial Beliefs

Learning what financial beliefs you have inherited from your ancestors is helpful because these beliefs may be getting in the way of you being financially successful. You may be in a cycle of subconscious sabotage! Some common beliefs that are not helpful:

- "Money is dirty."
- "It is unsafe to hold onto money."
- "Rich people are bad."
- "Money brings misery."
- "It is selfish to have money."
- "I must hang on to all my money."
- "I never have enough money."
- "I don't deserve money."
- "People use me for my money."

…And the list is endless. It is essential to take the time and effort to examine your beliefs about money; this will be a game-changer. I also encourage meeting with financial advisors to learn how to manage and save money to set yourself up for success.

Choosing new beliefs that support you in having success in the financial arena is imperative to change how you interact with money. Remember, money is only energy, a means to exchange goods and services. Ask anyone about their beliefs concerning money, and you will find a vast ocean of belief systems associated with money. Learning to manage money and disconnect from old beliefs that no longer serve you may take time and additional support. I encourage you to start mindfully changing your conversation about money and start with affirmations every day.

Money affirmation suggestions:

- "Money comes to me with ease."
- "I am grateful how money always shows up when I need it."
- "Money can help me heal and grow by using it toward classes or helping others."
- "Money can be used to help our environment."
- "It is safe to have money." Look for therapists with CMAT behind their name as they have financial disorders training.

Therapist training for financial disorders suggestion:
IITAP CMAT: https://iitap.com/page/CMAT

Memories about money

My beliefs about money

Affirmations to change beliefs

Surrender to the
JOURNEY

You are already on your path just by being conscious in the present moment and appreciating all that you have overcome. By believing this moment is an important part of your journey and continuing to focus on what brings you joy, you will bring more joy to the surface. Surrender to believing you are where you need to be to learn what you need to learn.

Channeling your purpose by visualizing more of what creates passion within you will help you take steps toward manifesting more of what you want in your life. Give yourself the time and space to brainstorm and develop in your "creation station" and notice what feels exciting.

Do you feel passionate about what you do? Do you look forward to going to work? If not, I suggest considering a change of occupation in the future. This can start with taking some classes and volunteering for different organizations to get a feel for what you are passionate about. You can find a mentor to speak with about an interest to develop a guide to where you want to go. Do you need a degree, experience, or training to make this change? Meditate and brainstorm to help discover answers that feel true and make daily small goals towards change. Change is less overwhelming when we break it down one step at a time. You will find the motivation to change as you tune into your passion and allow it to guide you! Create energy with passion and surrender when you are connected to passion, love, and joy, knowing you are being guided in the right direction.

Have faith in your journey and begin to blow the ceiling off your potential.

Playbook Activity:
Allow yourself to believe that you are right where you need to be, trusting that the struggles and challenges in your life have delivered you the wisdom and strength you need for your journey here on earth. Take a moment to be thankful for your entire life, not just the joy but all of it. Notice if your perspective changes when you view challenges as gifts for growth instead of viewing them as negative events.

Challenging Event

What I learned

How I grew

Understand these truths:
You are creative!
You are important!
You are meant to be here!

Be Limitless In Your Creativity

It is time to take the lid off your creativity and go big! Let yourself start brainstorming about what you want, visualize it happening daily, and look for the doors opening; they will. You can begin by trusting that you were meant to shine and that the universe has your back. We were not meant to play small, stay silent, or hide in the shadows. Let your heart guide you and go forward with the understanding of not harm. Please speak your truth and ask for help, pray for direction, and stay open to the guidance that comes to you. It will; don't expect it to show up exactly as you picture it.

Could you allow some creativity here? It may even be a minor disaster. Which may be the motivation to propel you forward and make long-term changes. You may ask for help from some people you think would want to lend a hand and instead find the opposite. Some people may even belittle you for asking for help and having big ambitions but don't give up. You are building your team!

Could you allow help to arrive in a different form than expected? Help may look like becoming inspired to collaborate with others or motivation to try a new approach to something old that you already knew how to do. Sometimes, it is just changing how something operates or switching perspectives by finding more user-friendly ways to operate a business. This forward-thinking has helped entrepreneurs make millions (look at Uber, Amazon, and Netflix) open to answers and allow them to appear. Imagination and play are great ways to stimulate creativity and create new doors where you once believed there were just old walls! I listen to Solex AO Scan, inner voice, calms my mind, and I find this helps me enter into a creative space. You can learn more about Solex, AO Scan, and inner voice scan with the link below:
https://www.solexglobal.com/innervoice
My page: https://shop.solexnation.com/RiaFlanagan/home

Playbook Activity:
What is your favorite visualization that you can recreate today?

Can you start imagining it becoming a reality? If not, what is in your way, and what is a creative solution to remove the block (ex. a tractor pulls up and physically removes it)?

Has it changed from day one? (The changes come from being more connected to your intuition and body, so you know more of what you want instead of what you thought you wanted.) Track changes as a way to know yourself better:

Sometimes, we could dream someone else's dream and not realize it. This happens from conditioning over time in dysfunctional family systems and toxic cultures. It is very freeing to cultivate your original, unique dream. You do this by staying connected to your emotions during visualization activities (stay playful and have fun).

Oxygen Mask
Are you rescuing everyone else and abandoning yourself?

If you were conditioned to be in the hero role in your family of origin, you may live your life with a sense of responsibility and obligation. Overworking and consistently trying to win validation from your boss, coworkers, family members, and partners, overextending yourself to help others and then being resentful. If you receive the validation, you may feel great momentarily. Still, unfortunately, if your ultimate belief is that it is your duty to care for and rescue others at the risk of your own mental and physical health, you will lose your authentic self and your purpose. Ultimately, if you are caught in this cycle, you may notice feeling depleted and resentful because you are not putting the oxygen mask on first. When you step away, ask yourself, "What do I need?" and "What do I want?" This is a start to living differently. Work on improving your self-care boundaries, like saying no when your energy is depleted and noticing how this is a step away from carrying resentments. Reflecting on how you may have been conditioned to neglect your own wants and needs with a counselor or coach can help create a deeper understanding of how family roles are created in dysfunctional family systems and do not serve you in living a happy life. This is not to say that we will always be happy or not to help others; it is just to say not to do it at the risk of losing yourself. I am grateful for all the frontline healthcare workers who support our community daily, and it is so important that they rest and take time for self-care at the end of a day's work.

When stuck in a hero role, you may give off the impression that others need to be saved by you. You become a magnet to attract people who are struggling in their own dysfunctional family role, maybe the "lost child" who is wounded from childhood abandonment or abuse. Consider how your rescuing may enable them to stay sick rather than becoming empowered, which may involve seeing a professional. Rescuers fall into roles in relationships of parent, cop, and superior, creating an imbalance in friendships and romantic relationships that destroys intimacy.

Playbook Activity:
Complete the scale and brainstorm different ways to increase meeting basic needs to create a more balanced lifestyle (Ex., add daily 30-minute exercise, weekly friend meetups, try a new hobby.)

Check off where you are on a percentage scale for satisfaction in meeting basic needs in your life: (0 is not meeting need, 5 is meeting need at approximately 50% or half the time, 10 is meeting this need at 100% all the time:

NEED	SCALE
1) Sleep:	0 1 2 3 4 5 6 7 8 9 10
2) Play:	0 1 2 3 4 5 6 7 8 9 10
3) Diet:	0 1 2 3 4 5 6 7 8 9 10
4) Exercise:	0 1 2 3 4 5 6 7 8 9 10
5) Quiet time:	0 1 2 3 4 5 6 7 8 9 10
6) Work life:	0 1 2 3 4 5 6 7 8 9 10
6) Relationships:	0 1 2 3 4 5 6 7 8 9 10
7) Hobbies:	0 1 2 3 4 5 6 7 8 9 10
8) Vacations:	0 1 2 3 4 5 6 7 8 9 10

Think of this balancing act of life as a see-saw, and the priorities constantly change depending on the specific ups and downs. If you didn't get a good night's sleep, you may need to prioritize your diet and ease up on work that day to help keep the rhythm going. Change is constant, but if you move to the beat and shuffle your feet, you can keep from falling off the see-saw (Ex. overworking, poor diet).

What is the priority today to keep the rhythm moving?

Honoring Our WORTH

Worth is inherent; no one can truly give it to you or take it from you. You are born worthy.

We are all worthy, and we were born this way. No one can take it from us, though trauma can impact our beliefs, making us believe we are not worthy. Healing is about returning to the authentic self and connecting to your mind, body, and soul (connection to all life). When you are integrating all three, this is where truth lives, and our inner knowing can affirm... "You are worthy, always were, and will always be!" This concept is infinite, but we tend to perceive things as right or wrong, concrete instead of fluid, where there must be a winner and a loser. We tend to miss all the win-win options. Blind to see the infinite colors and shapes, living in chaos and fear, caught in the struggle of proving we are right and the other is wrong. How peaceful would it be now if you let yourself believe you are worthy? How would your life change? What would you do differently? Today, try living "as if" you believe you are worthy; wear it like a crown. Notice the feeling of this, to live in a place where you have unconditional love as you are, and no one can take it from you. This is a spiritual concept! Now, look at everyone else and see them as just as worthy. How would we interact differently with the world and ourselves? If you can act as if long enough, it will seep in... It can transform you!

Playbook Activity:
How would your life be different if you truly believed you were worthy and a miracle? If you like the answer, start affirming yourself at least 500 times a day: "I am worthy" until you believe it. How can you model it to support others if you know you are worthy?

Tips: Every time you walk through a doorway, affirm yourself 5 times in your mind, or while you are working out, write affirmations on a fun sticky note, post them on your bathroom mirror, and repeat affirmations daily until they become a belief about yourself. Check back in two weeks and write out, "I believe am..."

Book suggestions: Facing Codependence and
Facing Love Addiction - By Pia Mellody

LIFE IS A MIRACLE AND SO ARE YOU!

Magic and Wonder is for adults too

Remember being a child and believing in magic? It is when we lose touch with our creative spirit, our inner child, that we forget we are magic. We lose the ability to see all the miracles everywhere when we focus on what is not working in our world. It is easy to do when fear is created through the news and with social media locking us into a fear-based life. Spend some time in quiet; meditate to open yourself up to the magic that is you. Start looking for what is working in the world and in your life and all the people dedicated to helping heal the planet and themselves! Living in gratitude and making an effort to thank others around us is key to tapping into this energy that may in itself be just another word for magic. If you made it this far in this course, notice we are building a foundation – a new way of thinking and being!

When you see the beauty in yourself, you will see it everywhere. When I hold my baby girl, who I know is a miracle, I ask myself why I think I am not a miracle, and then I come back to the truth… We are all miracles. It is easy to stop seeing the miracles as we become busy adults, surviving day-to-day life of family, work, children, attaining goals, errands, paying bills, meeting obligations, trying to self-care, and on and on it goes! In this chaos, it is so important to slow down and be in nature; watch the sunset, the ocean waves rolling to the shore, sit and notice the wildlife, and the genius of nature. The miracles are everywhere if you stop to notice them and get out of your own way. What are some new possibilities in your life you have overlooked? What are some current blessings you have not opened your eyes to? Notice doors open as you allow them to. Witness the miracles from a state of child-like wonder. The miracles are everywhere.

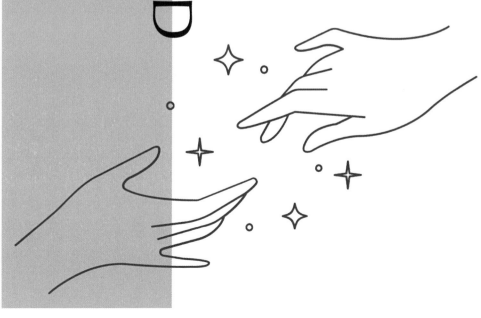

Playbook Activity:
Notice some miracles happening right now. Write down
several. It could be as simple as breathing...

Learn how to have self-compassion in your daily life. I know you are doing your best, but why don't you know it? Stop any negative self-talk in its tracks and picture yourself kicking the bully out of the room. Now replace the bully with an angelic guide, a best friend, or a cheerleader, and have them give you a powerful pep talk about how amazing you are! Try it, I guarantee you will have a better day hanging out with this best friend instead of the negative bully trying to run the show.

Negative self-talk can often shut us down, lower motivation, and push us into a shame spiral where we end up getting nothing done. Choosing self-compassion allows us space to breathe, time to heal, and motivation to get back up and keep working toward our goals. Change the voice in your mind and change your life. Be mindful to replace the negative talk with self-compassion and nurturing and start to notice things change. I often encourage my clients to picture their adult selves, rescuing their younger selves from being bullied. This can feel empowering, and doing inner child work with a therapist can be a way to start tapping into and practicing self-compassion.

If you grew up in a household where emotions were suppressed and a "suck it up" attitude was enforced, it may take some coaching to be comfortable with having self-compassion. If you view your past with compassion and love, would things be different?

Try reframing all the hard times as being an essential part of your journey. Begin offering yourself grace. Showing yourself grace can be challenging, so let's work through that on the next page.

Self-Compassion is Grace

Try to slow down today, and any moment you feel critical of yourself, stop and write a new dialogue written by your best friend, loving family member, guardian angel, mentor, or inspirational figure. Have this dialogue help you transform how you show up for yourself and empower yourself to live up to your potential. The truth is, when we have the support to thrive, we thrive!

Book Suggestions: Self-Compassion by Kristine Neff PH.D.

Playbook Activity:
Pick a situation in your life you are critical of yourself in. Now, practice instead having self-compassion around the situation and notice how the feelings change. Where else in your life can you replace the inner critic with self-compassion?

Write out a new dialogue for yourself that is self-compassionate about one or two situations. Read them back to yourself. Write out and track any changes in emotion here. Give yourself a high 5, you are making progress!

Slow down... Make time for grace

Like the directions of most recipes say, "Add a dash of salt," it is time to add a dash of daily grace to your life. We have lived through a pandemic where most of the world had moments of shutting down. Giving ourselves grace is essential at this time. We may need a break, a holiday, or a mental health day from work to calm down our nervous system. How can you slow down and allow a moment of space in your daily activity to practice grace for yourself and others? The world needs this right now; it has been a difficult year for human beings. Just pause from your weekly routine and have some fun. Give yourself grace with a daily reminder that you are doing your best, and that is all you can do. Once you start giving yourself more grace, next make a point to also pay it forward by being kind to the checkout clerk, the waitress, your health care professional, spouse, child, sibling, friend, co-worker, parents, and everyone who crosses your path because it has been tough to be a human. We all deserve a dash of grace in our day! Being a graceful person will surely have you lighting up a room.

Emotions Light Up the Room

I love children's books and stories that say we are made from stardust. We are energy, we are light, and energy can be transformed, just like emotions can be transformed when they are processed. We often suppress or ignore uncomfortable emotions like fear, pain, shame, and guilt and lose the messages from the emotions that are trying to provide growth, awareness, protection, and healing. You can begin changing how you react to your emotions by actively allowing them to pass through you, visualizing them moving like clouds or waves, and tuning into the messages they have for you. Acknowledge these emotions by breathing into them, and be open to the gifts they came to teach you.

Allowing yourself the mindfulness to receive the growth, wisdom, protection, and healing they were meant to provide you. It is when we stuff our emotions that we can end up feeling anxious or depressed. When we suppress or numb our emotions, we lose the lessons and growth they are trying to provide us, which stunts our development.

This developmental delay creates issues with reactivity, immaturity, lack of insight, and poor decision-making. If we stop judging emotions as good or bad and start to witness that the emotions are just energy, and can move through us like a ray of light being transformed into wisdom and growth. This way of processing emotions can become easy and natural with some practice.

Playbook Activity:
Write each feeling you had this week, take some deep breaths, and sit with your emotions. Ask yourself what you think the wisdom or gift this feeling brought you...

1) I felt love when...

The gift of this emotion may be...

2) I felt passion when...

The gift of this emotion may be...

3) I felt sadness when...

The gift of this emotion may be...

4) I felt fear today when...

The gift of this emotion may be...

5) I felt angry today when...

The gift of anger may be...

6) I felt guilt today when...

The gift of guilt may be...

7) I felt shame today when...

The gift of shame may be...

The frequency of LOVE

We can choose to let go of holding on to fear and start this process by channeling loving thoughts; "I am supported by the universe," "I can choose to be at peace," or "I am safe, loved, and protected." Everything has a frequency.

We attract more love in our lives as we work on being comfortable with receiving love. How do you push intimacy away and wall off from others trying to connect to you? When focused on the fear of being hurt, we are paralyzed and walled off from love. When living a fear-based life, we always try to control everything and not trust in our journey. We become frozen in our fear-based beliefs, thinking that others will only hurt us. Practicing letting go of fear may entail getting help from a therapist or treatment team if it has become a debilitating habit. If your nervous system is so severely offline that you are out of touch with joy and peace, it may mean you need more support to heal past trauma. It is also essential to assess if the fear is real and try to alert you to danger. If it is an old fear you have not yet let go of, you probably need help processing it completely. Living in fear can escalate into obsessions and leave a person feeling isolated and unable to trust others or connect fully. Often, attending therapy to process through trauma can help if you feel stuck in fear. The Power of Now by Eckhart Tolle is a helpful book for tuning into the present moment. Noticing that you made it through the difficult times in the past and are no longer that person and are no longer in that situation helps you focus on the present (Tolle, 2009) You are lovable and safe! Check out, the love frequency 528Hertz, on YouTube: https://www.youtube.com/watch?v=ILQ7lEhpfjc

I love using frequencies to help regulate the nervous system. I offer the Safe and Sound Protocol (SSP) to clients, which is music with specific frequencies to contribute to feeling safe in the body created by Dr. Stephen Porges, you can read about the sciene on the Untye website: https://integratedlistening.com/polyvagal-theory/

I have witnessed clients report significant lower levels of anxiety within 30 days

Playbook Activity:
Visualize moving a current situation that feels stuck by
expanding the sensations of love like the sun melting ice
(somatic technique). How would the situation change?

As I visualize the situation
with unconditional love...

The situation now
starts to look like ...

How I visualize the situation
changing for the best
outcome for everyone?

Respect
Diversity, Equity, and Inclusion

We teach others how to treat us by what we are willing to tolerate. I encourage you to start believing in your badass self now. Book suggestion for feeling like a badass: "You Are a Badass" by Jen Sincero. If you have not yet arrived at this place of believing you are fantastic, start acting as if you think that you are an incredible, miraculous human. One way to start doing this is by practicing inclusivity and equality. This means taking zero s*** from bullies, including the bullies in your head. We can wall people out due to our own insecurities and fears. Do not stand for insults, condescension, or abuse in any form. Stand up for what is right without violence and anger but with intention and love. Be strong in your vulnerability and courageous in your growth. Learn about gaslighting and stop the cycle. Treat everyone with equal respect. Begin with respecting your health and well-being. Stay out of drama and gossip. We can be peaceful in this process by setting healthy boundaries with others and not remaining in unhealthy relationships. Learn how to be supportive to others without harming yourself or putting your mental health at risk! Take judgment off of the table. Learn how to listen by being fully present with others instead of offering up opinions. Listening is a skill we can all learn to master by tuning in to the other person and letting go of what we think the other will say. We become of valuable service to another person when we can hold a judgmental-free space for them. By allowing others a safe place to share their thoughts and feelings without trying to fix or solve their issues, we begin to allow intimacy, safety, and connection in our relationships. If you are in recovery or curious about recovery and want a fresh DEI approach, check out Andi Wiseman's book, The Unsuble Art of Unf*cking Your Life.

VIEW EVERYONE AS WORTHY AND LOVABLE

genders ages disabilities justice employment inclusion ethnicities genders
inclusion diversity society ages cultures equity abilities
justice employment ages fairness opportunity religions inclusion diversity justice religions respect
justice genders equity fairness inclusion sexual orientations
employment races cultures respect cultures society equity ages ages equity inclusion opportunity cultures respect society diversity abilities
society genders society justice genders abilities ages fairness respect

DEI DIVERSITY EQUITY INCLUSION

genders disabilities inclusion abilities respect society opportunity inclusion cultures fairness justice employment equity
fairness religions abilities abilities opportunity
inclusion society diversity abilities equity justice disabilities races
religions respect equity fairness society

1) Think of 5 people who inspire you and write down the characteristics that stand out in these people.

2) Now visualize yourself in your creation station having conversations with each of them.

3) Write out several questions you want to ask these mentors.

4) Brainstorm a dialogue with these mentors responding to your questions.

RISE UP & SHINE

When you settle for a job, relationship, or living space that you don't really love – as I am pretty sure from my own life experience – it will haunt you in one way or another. You are worthy of a fantastic life! Hold out for the job you are passionate about and the relationship of your dreams, and keep looking until you find the house and place you can be blissful in. If you have not started a vision board to help visualize your best life, the time is now. We can all get stuck in a place of survival, doing what we have to do to get to the next day. To thrive, we have to choose to change things to move to the next level of this game called life. You got this. Do you know how I know? Because you are here and present at this moment. Staying present is the start of noticing how you can create a beautiful life. The actor Jim Carrey shared his visualization story on Oprah in 1997. He shared about when he was a struggling actor, he wrote a check to himself for 10 million dollars and kept it in his wallet for years when he barely had enough money for gas. Finally, the day came when he found out he would make around 10 million for the film Dumb and Dumber.

1) Visualization is powerful
2) Be mindful and connected to joy, passion, and love when you visualize the next chapter of your life!
Believe you deserve this happiness.

Never Settle For Less

Jim Carrey initially believed happiness would be found when becoming a rich and famous movie star, and manifested this dream through hard work and visualization. A twist in the story is that Mr. Carrey later shares that this dream of fame and fortune did not make him happy. In his quest for happiness after fame and fortune, he found Transcendental Meditation (TM). Other famous people known for practicing meditation are Jerry Seinfeld, Katy Perry, Tom Hanks, Oprah Winfrey, Lady Gaga, Sir Paul McCartney, Hugh Jackman, and Arianna Huffington (Natale & Welch, 2024). Connecting to a life with purpose is a way to infuse passion on the journey. Knowing your true, authentic self is the most crucial chapter to uncover; everything else will reveal itself when you truly know yourself.

Happiness is not found outside of you, but it is found within. Remember, everything outside of you is fleeting. Your job, relationship, family, and material things can all be taken away, so if this is how you found peace, it is transient and can be taken away quickly.

Playbook Activity:
Make a list of 10 to 20 internal things that bring you joy. Next, start to focus more attention on how to grow and nurture these areas in your life!

Create your FATE

Remember that you always have the choice to change jobs, partners, or yourself. I found that until I worked on myself, changing the other things in my life did not make much of a difference. I encourage everyone to dig deep and work on finding peace within themselves; then, the rest will fall into place. When we make things and people our source of happiness, we will become challenged if any of those things outside sources of happiness go away.

When we learn to master ourselves, listen to our emotions, and trust our intuition, we become free. Freedom is trusting our choices and living in truth without regret or resentment. When we hand our well-being over to outside sources, we are living chained to these sources. Become the narrator of your life, dream the most exciting dream, and become the magician who makes it happen. I know this is possible because I have challenged myself, beat the odds and now I can help others do the same.

We must break any patterns of victim thinking and take responsibility to become our own champian in our life to leave a legacy when we go. We have all had some pain or trauma at some point in life (we are living in a world where it can be heartbreaking to listen to the news, trauma is unavoidable), but trauma can be healed, and it is crucial to get help to heal. As adults, we are responsible for getting the support we need to heal.

Hurt people, hurt people. Do not let the perpetrator, the traumatic event, or circumstance steal your whole life. Ask for help, be your own hero by accepting support, practicing vulnerability, and taking risks to live your life in a state of passion and love, instead of hiding in fear. You are worth it. Do not give your power away; the past does not define you. In fact, it is proof of how amazing, brave, and courageous you were to overcome it!

Notice how many choices you have, that you have the power to decide every day how to be in the world. You could choose to be empowered to contribute to an important cause. You are never stuck; some people in jail find ways to internalize peace through the power of their minds, so it is possible for all of us. Choose your thoughts today. Make this a day of connection to self and others, and send love to everyone you encounter; trust me, we could all use more love in our lives. Notice the positive difference this can make in your day, and keep doing it!

Movie suggestion: "Life is Beautiful" - directed by Roberto Benigni

Playbook Activity:

What is an important cause you would feel
empowered contributing to (ex: clean water, feeding
the homeless, animal shelters, foster children?

Cause:

What amount of time, energy or funding would feel good for
you and be manageable for you today, weekly, monthly?

Amount of time, energy, funds today:

Amount of time, energy, funds weekly:

Amount of time, energy, funds monthly:

Write out how it feels to be part of a nobel cause ...
Sit with it... soak in it... expand it with breath...

Reflection:

Ripple Effect
We are all connected!

Imagine what you could do for humanity, the earth, and the starving if you had a billion dollars. During this recent pandemic, the world was impacted; we have all been touched in one way or another. When we live in a way that is consciously harmonious and in alignment with what is best for all humanity, we heal not only ourselves but we contribute to healing our planet and those we love. We really cannot fix anyone else, but when we live our best lives, we influence and create ripples in the water that impact others. When we buy a recycled product or recycle, we work towards the solution. When we spend a couple of extra dollars to buy organic or give to a charity at the grocery store, we are in the energy of hope, charity, and healing the planet instead of contributing to toxins that are destroying it.

Whatever the cause is you are passionate about, be it saving the bees, helping refugees in Afghanistan, fostering children without families, or volunteering at an animal shelter... Whatever you are passionate about, start to be a part of helping a cause other than just yourself. It is empowering to be part of the solution and rewarding to give others love. Take a moment and look at how abundant we all are living, breathing, and dreaming. With all the freedoms that others have fought and died for. Now it may be your turn to find your way of giving back to the others who have fought for you. Trust me, this is one of the best investments anyone can make. Having extra bottled water in your car when driving to work to give to a homeless person (In Arizona, you may have saved them from a hospital visit), taking your family every couple of months to help feed the homeless, or raising money for a charitable cause. Another way to give back is to offer your service to a charitable cause, volunteer for The Red Cross, or work with veterans, the homeless, or children in group homes.

What can you do today to help someone in need? Notice how much you have in your life that you are able to help another person or cause. Allow yourself to be a part of changing the world and notice how empowering this is. You can make a difference.

Our Actions have a Ripple effect

Playbook Activity:
Brainstorm things you care about (nature, clean
water, feeding hungry children)...

What ways can you contribute to helping
(charity, volunteer, advocate, recycle)?

We are capable of connecting deeply in transformative ways

Bob Dylan sang about how we all have to "serve somebody." What if we re-frame our perspective so we can be in gratitude when we get to be a part of helping someone on their journey. Try changing your perspective on doing things you may normally avoid, like paying bills, sending a quick "Thank you" to the universe for having the credit to afford a place to live, and creditors that trust you. When we have faith in our path, trusting that money is just energy that comes and goes as we need it, we tip better and become more charitable. Entering out of a state of lack and into a state of trust, things move easier, and we become unstuck. We all end up serving someone, so why not do it in a space of joy and gratitude! We enter a state of empowerment when we consciously move toward service of another. We are capable of helping and supporting one another if we are open and passionate about it!

Notice if you are contributing to the separation of others from yourself. In what areas of your life do you judge others as wrong and yourself as right? I encourage you to be curious about other people's perceptions and how they were developed. Next, spend some time questioning your own beliefs. Were your beliefs inherited, or did you create them from experience? See what it is like to agree to disagree instead of having to be correct and make others wrong. Try serving another person by really listening to them, tuning in with curiosity instead of listening to respond. Thank them for sharing, and after, notice if your connection deepens.

Whom can you become curious about today?

What would be interesting to know about them?

Get curious when this person shares who they are and notice how it feels to connect deeper. Write out some reflections on this connection as you deepen it:

Live with Integrity

"The greatness of a man is not in how much wealth he acquires but in his integrity and his ability to affect those around him positively." – Bob Marley

Living with integrity is about keeping your word, being honest, and treating people kindly. You create a reputation for yourself through your credibility, your lifelong friends, the way you conduct business, and how you treat people in general.

Do you speak to the cashier at your grocery store and your server at a restaurant the same way you speak to your boss, or do you treat people differently?

Do you keep to your word, or do you overcommit and underperform? Do you follow through with promises and things you have agreed to? It is important to be true to your word so people can trust you. Would you trust you?

Where has trust been broken in our lives? Where have we broken trust?

Building back trust can be a long road where actions must align with the words spoken

Playbook Activity:
Completion

Start with yourself; what are you willing to commit to today and follow through with (working out, following up with a friend, completing a project)?

Make space
for your happiness...

When the time is right, the students will become the masters. One day, I hope we all realize it is an incredible honor to share gifts and experiences and help others live their best lives. Mentoring another human is a fantastic experience. Before taking on another commitment, always ensure you give only what you have to offer. Ensure your boundaries are clear and you stick to them. Model healthy boundaries by communicating expectations clearly and maintaining healthy self-care. It is critical to only give what you have the energy for. If you feel resentful or exhausted by over-giving, it may be a sign to set boundaries and communicate your wants and needs to create a win-win situation instead of a win-lose. This may look like managing your time and schedule differently to manage your priorities. Self-care is not an option but a necessity if you want to be successful in creating more happiness. This means self-care is a priority, and you may need to increase your time for yourself before committing to someone else. When you have not made the time to create space for happiness, you are vulnerable to living someone else's version of what happiness is and losing sight of what truly makes you happy.

I am honored you completed this journey with me, and I hope your playbook activities guided you to increase your happiness levels! Keep doing what works! All our journeys are unique; be true to you!

CONCLUSION

Playbook Activity:
Don't play small shine brightly!

Brainstorm a superhero self if you play small that you can shine brightly in, and write about how this would feel different. The next time you are in a difficult situation, visualize wearing this hero as a suit of armor to help you overcome life's challenges. You are the superhero of your own life! You have got this!

Express Yourself

Express yourself in words, in art, in movement, share the highs and lows of life, be authentic, be flawed, be famous or infamous, be a recluse or a rebel, and maybe for a time, you try on different superhero costumes until you realize the only person who needs saving is you. You are the one you have been searching for... As we walk our path, we inevitably fall down and experience the hard landings. People will gaslight, betray, rob, and perhaps cheat and lie to our faces with the most convincing arguments. Remember that it is not about you. That is about who they are; our work is not to take it personally. We will all experience some heartbreak, be it the death of a loved one, unexpected breakups, a dream left behind, a friend that moved away when you needed them most, a broken system, loving someone who cannot love you back, losing a job, changing careers, a friend or lover ghosts you, realizing your parents are flawed or your fantasy relationship does not exist. We will ride the waves of emotions, and though it may feel like we are lost in the ocean storm, we manage to swim to shore, hanging on the lifeboats of our support systems, the true friends, and family, and that inner life force that helps us take another breath. I am grateful for you being here and reading this! I hope I was able to pass on some of the wisdom I have gained from the hard falls and the heartbreak.

Creating a greater capacity to feel and hold the sensations of happiness is a practice. A daily intention to receive and allow this emotion, giving conscious permission to yourself that you are worthy of joy, that it was meant for you. Understand that feeling all the emotions will deepen your gratitude when you dance with the sensations of joy, passion, and love. We are not one dimension, we are many layers, complex and wonderful, we are relatable to one another through our diverse range of emotions and choosing to allow more happiness is a choice I hope you make for yourself! Much love for you on this wild, wonderous life path!

What is the Intention you want to create for yourself for the next chapter of your adventure...See you in the next Playbook!

REFERENCES

Adobe Stock Photos, Thomsond, Faiza, Bedaniel, Carden, K., spirit, A., Jeanette, PITTYAHA, Lazy_Bear, jin, V., Panyawatt, Ödön, C., Bisams, BeDoa, Kanisorn, Studioworkstock, Kardaska, Summit Art Creation, Freshidea,...Baarssen, F. (2024). 627348325, 358512284, 313092330, 788988332, 635522931, 253391891, 141328113, 723124498, 772404260, 563538348, 765330086, 625711037, 727230729, 522903146, 729727950, 704559327, 737979787, 724377313, 783561619, 383166703, 7 06374232, 750825395, 673420035, 732196040, 716045424, 781661255, 718731475, 48146969, 613259242, 769294604, 793744161, 762412364, 801569657, 683703649, 385051241, 714723859, 205071998, 815175772, 558002179, 419215204, 737496157, 816389413, 693091509, 203057102 [Photo]. Adobe Stock Photos. https://stock.adobe.com/Dashboard/LicenseHistory

Becker, G. D. (1997). Gift of fear. Bloomsbury Publishing PLC.

Belic, R. (Director). (2012). Happy [Film]. https://www.imdb.com/title/tt1613092/?ref_=nm_knf_i_3

Benigni, R., Braschi, N., Gori, M. C., Gori, V. C., Cerami, V., Ferri, E., & Braschi, G. (2000). Life is beautiful. Miramax Home Entertainment.

Black, C. (2018). A hole in the sidewalk: The recovering person's guide to relapse prevention. Central Recovery Press.

Black, C. (2024). Undaunted hope (1st ed.). Central Recovery Press, LLC.

Brené Brown, Ph.D., L.M.S.W. (2014). Gifts of imperfection, the (Unabridged ed.). Brilliance Audio.

Brickman, P., Coates, D., & Janoff-Bulman, R. (1978). Lottery winners and accident victims: Is happiness relative? Journal of Personality and Social Psychology, 36(8), 917–927. Retrieved May 5, 2024, from https://doi.org/10.1037//0022-3514.36.8.917

Byrne, R. (2016). Rhonda byrne 4 books bundle collection (the magic,the power,hero,the secret). Lenka Tulenka.

Cameron, J. (1995). The artist's way. Pan.

Canva. (2024a). Table of contents 4 [AI generator oon Canva].

Canva. (2024b, April 26). Balancing Scales [AI generater in Canva]. https://www.canva.com/design/DAF_nBJHvhU/0haN8MWbMrB7ISXyqp0K6A/edit

Canva & Flanagan, R. (2024a). Rescuer hero. Canva. https://www.canva.com/design/DAF_nBJHvhU/0haN8MWbMrB7ISXyqp0K6A/edit

Canva & Flanagan, R. (2024b). Table of contents 3 [AI generater on Canva].

Canva & Flanagan, R. (2024c, April 25). Illustration for Happiness is an inside Playbook [AI generated]. Canva. https://www.canva.com/design/DAGDjHYzFFE/oytzLEDBbARMXaVwK77p_A/edit

Canva & Flanagan, R. (2024a, April 26). Lost Child [AI Generated]. CANVA. https://www.canva.com/design/DAF_nBJHvhU/0haN8MWbMrB7ISXyqp0K6A/edit

Canva & Flanagan, R. (2024b, April 26). Sailboat on peaceful ocean [AI generated]. CANVA. https://www.canva.com/design/DAF_nBJHvhU/0haN8MWbMrB7ISXyqp0K6A/edit Csikszentmihalyi, M. (2022). Flow.

Daly, S. (2015). The body keeps the score van der kolk bessel the body keeps the score 443pp £25 penguin 9780241003985 0241003989. Emergency Nurse, 22(10), 12–12. https://doi.org/10.7748/en.22.10.12.s13

Docter, P., & Del Carmen, R. (Directors). (2015). Inside Out [Film].

Dyer, W. W. (2008). You'll see it when you believe it. HarperCollins.

Emdr basic training. (2024). EMDR International Association. Retrieved January 28, 2024, from https://www.emdria.org/emdr-training/

Gabor, M. M. (2022). The myth of normal: Trauma, illness, and healing in a toxic culture. Avery.

Gracey, M. (Director). (2021). Pink: All I Know So Far [Film].

Huffington, A. (2015). Thrive: The third metric to redefining success and creating a life of well-being, wisdom, and wonder (Reprint ed.). Harmony.

Kondō, M. (2014). The life-changing magic of tidying up: The Japanese art of decluttering and organizing (1st ed.). Ten Speed Press.

Lee, J. (2001). Growing yourself back up (1st ed.). Harmony.

Levine, P. A. (2017). Waking the tiger. Tantor Media Inc.

Martela, F., Laitinen, E., & Hakulinen, C. (2024). Which predicts longevity better: Satisfaction with life or purpose in life? Psychology and Aging. Retrieved May 6, 2024, from https://doi.org/10.1037/pag0000802

Mellody, P. (2011). Facing love addiction. HarperCollins Publishers.

Mellody, P. (2024). All of the Feels: Accepting the Gifts of Emotion [Eight Basic Emotions]. Claudia Black: Young Adult Center. Retrieved April 16, 2024, from

Mellody, P., Miller, A. W., & Miller, J. K. (2011). Facing codependence. Harper Collins.

Millman, D. (2000). The life you were born to live (Later Printing ed.). Mjf Books.

Neff, K. (2011). Self compassion. Hodder & Stoughton.

Newton, T., & Gallagher, J. R. (2019). Unspoken legacy. Alcoholism Treatment Quarterly, 38(2), 286–287. Retrieved May 7, 2024, from https://doi.org/10.1080/07347324.2019.1611398

Patel, A. (2019). Programs - tree of life success series - choose your point of entry! Tree of Life Success Series. Retrieved May 7, 2024, from https://www.treeoflifesuccess.com/programs/

Patel, A. (2024). Evolve - tree of life success series - signature program. Tree of Life Success Series. Retrieved May 14, 2024, fromhttps://www.treeoflifesuccess.com/evolve/?_gl=1*1liue7y*_up*MQ..*_ga*MjY2NTM2NTM1LjE3MTU3MDI2NDE.*_ga_Q6LHX2ZX8H*MTcxNTcwMjY0MS4xLjEuMTcxNTcwMjY2OC4wLjAuMA..

Schwartz, & Richard. (2023). No bad parts. Vermilion.

Shetty, J. (n.d.). Think like a monk new (gujrati).

ShniDesign, S. (2024). 683703649 [AI Photo]. Adobe Stock Photos. https://stock.adobe.com/Dashboard/LicenseHistory

Sincero, J. (2016). You are a badass. John Murray Learning.

Somatic Experiencing International. (2024). About - somatic experiencing® international. Somatic Experiencing® International. Retrieved February 8, 2024, from https://traumahealing.org/about/

Supplemental material for happiness—to enjoy now or later? consequences of delaying happiness and living in the moment beliefs. (2021). Emotion. Retrieved May 6, 2024, from https://doi.org/10.1037/emo0000850.supp

Tolle, E. (2009). The power of now. Hachette Livre Australia.

Weis, B. L. (2015). Meditations [Speech audio recording]. Weiss Institute.

Wiseman, A. (2024). The Unsubtle Art of Unf*cking Your Life (1st ed.). Amazon.

Printed in the United States
by Baker & Taylor Publisher Services